610.69 Seide, Diane
SEI
    Careers in medical
      science

DATE			

© THE BAKER & TAYLOR CO.

CAREERS IN MEDICAL SCIENCE

by
Diane Seide

THOMAS NELSON INC., PUBLISHERS
Nashville, Tennessee / New York, New York

Copyright © 1973 by Diane Seide

All rights reserved under International and Pan-American Conventions. Published by Thomas Nelson Inc., Nashville, Tennessee, and simultaneously in Don Mills, Ontario, by Thomas Nelson & Sons (Canada) Limited. Manufactured in the United States of America.

Second printing

Library of Congress Cataloging in Publication Data

Seide, Diane.
  Careers in medical science.

  SUMMARY: Describes such careers in the field of medicine as nursing, inhalation therapist, mental health technician, optometrist, psychiatric social worker, physician's assistant, and others. Includes addresses of schools and sources of further information.
  1. Medicine as a profession—Juvenile literature. [1. Medicine as a profession] I. Title. [DNLM: 1. Health occupations—Popular works. W21 S458c 1973]
R690.S45   610.69   73-13538
ISBN 0-8407-6312-3

Preface

I wish to express my gratitude to Elizabeth Cintron for providing me with a fresh insight into the way today's student nurse is working toward improved community health nursing standards. Elizabeth is an example of the young, aware, compassionate nurse who really cares about people and wants to serve their health needs.

I especially want to thank Gail Kelley of Mount Sinai Hospital's Health Career Program for her interest, time, and encouragement in the preparation of this manuscript. Professional women like Gail Kelley perform a most important task by giving high school students the kind of counseling they need to plan useful careers for their future—and the nation's.

The salaries and incomes given in this book are not intended to be definitive, since they will vary, depending on the part of the country, the type of community, and the size of the health facility. In some communities, salaries and incomes are considerably higher than those given; in some, they may be lower.

Diane Seide

For Michael and Sabrina

Contents

1. The World of the Hospital   11

2. The Lady with the Lamp   15
   Nursing   15
   The Urban Public Health Nurse   18

3. Microbe Sleuths   23
   The Certified Laboratory Assistant   27
   The Histology Technician   28
   The Cytotechnologist   28
   The Medical Technologist   29

4. The Breath of Life—The Inhalation Therapist   33

5. Those Who Walk in Darkness   41
   The Mental Health Technician   42
   The Psychiatric Social Worker   47

6. The Rehab Corps   51
   The Physical Therapist   51
   The Speech Therapist   54
   The Occupational Therapist   57
   The Recreation Therapist   59

7. The Rest of the Team   61
   The X-Ray Technician   61
   The Dietitian   62
   The Dental Hygienist   64
   The Medical Record Technician   65

CAREERS IN MEDICAL SCIENCE

      The Emergency Room Technician   66
      The Operating Room Technician   68

8. Climbing Up the Medical Ladder   70
      The Optometrist   70
      The Dentist   73
      The Physician's Assistant   74

9. The Most Noble Profession—The Doctor   80

10. The Practice of the Healing Art   97
      The Intern   97
      The Resident   98
      Specialization   100
      The Cardiac Surgeon   103
      The Transplant Surgeon   104
      Space Medicine   105

11. Your Place on the Team   109
      The Podiatrist   111
      The Public Health Statistician   112
      The Health Teacher   114
      The Pharmacist   116
      The Environmental Technician   117
      The Sanitarian   118
      The Biomedical Equipment Technician   119
      The Hospital Administrator   121

Appendix   124
      Your Personal Health Career
         Match-Mate Tests   124
      Handy Health Career Guide   128
      Complete Guide to Health Organizations   130
      Glossary of Terms and Abbreviations   136

Index   139

To know is science—to think you know is ignorance.

—Hippocrates

1.
The World of the Hospital

"Code 222! Code 222!"

The voice booms out over the P.A. system. Immediately a team of highly specialized physicians rushes to the E.R. (emergency room). The patient is a sixty-five-year-old man in cardiac arrest. He is lying on a stretcher, the big overhead light beating down on him. His skin is a dusky blue. Foam trickles out of the corner of his mouth.

An orderly has stripped off the man's clothes. A nurse is stationed at the arrest cart to draw upon emergency drugs, which will be needed quickly. The team goes into action.

An anesthesiologist starts resuscitation while another physician begins external heart massage. A nurse takes blood from a hand vein and sends it with a volunteer to the lab *stat*, hospital slang for "immediate." I.V.'s (intravenous tubes) are ready. A resident physician inserts an intracath into one of the patient's arm veins. Two more I.V.'s are started. The doctor calls for emergency drugs. A nurse checks the patient's pulse and blood pressure, and then two paddles, connected to an electric outlet, are positioned on the patient's chest on either side of the heart. The order to flip the switch of the defibrillator is given.

The Head Nurse snaps, "Stand clear!"

Everyone moves away from the edge of the stretcher as the electric current flows through the paddles and shocks the man's heart into life. An involuntary quiver flutters his chest wall. The doctors take cardiogram readings. A nurse arrives from the C.C.U. (cardiac care unit), with a special monitor, and the patient is hooked up to it.

"He's breathing," the chief resident murmurs, listening to the patient's heart sounds.

"Let's get him up to the C.C.U."

Outside in the jammed waiting room, the patient's wife and son are peering down the corridor, shifting from one foot to the other, wondering what is happening. The Head Nurse starts to go over to talk to them, but dozens of people—patients, social workers, clerks, student nurses—bombard her with questions. She patiently gives them instructions. Then she listens sympathetically for a few minutes to the mother and son.

Yes, she tells them, Mr. Cummings is very ill, but he is holding on. The doctors are going to transfer him to the cardiac care unit.

She reassures them as much as she can before being called to another emergency. A seventeen-year-old girl has just been brought in with an overdose....

In the O.R. (operating room) on the seventh floor, a surgeon is performing a kidney transplant, while in the room down the hall a famous heart surgeon is doing a four-way coronary bypass, always a tricky operation. Only the most skilled cardiac surgeon would attempt it.

Highly experienced nurses assist each surgeon; they have had special training for their jobs and are dedicated to serving the patients and doctors who rely upon them. The O.R. nurse knows and understands the burden of responsibility that the surgeon alone carries on his shoulders the moment he steps into the operating room.

At that same moment a baby is about to be born. It is

The World of the Hospital

the first baby for the young woman who is being wheeled into the delivery room. Her husband is with her. They have both taken a special course in the psychoprophylactic method of childbirth, and so are mentally prepared for the experience. So, like many fathers-to-be, the husband can now be present in the delivery room. He is an active participant, taking his proper place in the birth of his child, instead of playing the role of the chain-smoking cartoon character pacing the floor of the waiting room.

The mother-to-be lies on the table. She is coached in her breathing by a sensitive maternity nurse. The husband, wearing a green jump suit, mask, and cap, sits on a stool at the head of the table. He will be able to watch the delivery through a mirror at the foot of the table.

The nurse drapes a warm sterile blanket over the heated crib prepared for the baby. Oxygen and suction are ready for the child if needed. The nurse uncovers the sterile-instrument stands, while the obstetrician scrubs. He pokes his head in and encourages his patient.

Another contraction builds up. The patient breathes rapidly and shallowly. Her husband gives her support by praising her efforts. She breathes deeply several times as the contraction ends. Her hair leaves a damp ring on the blue sheet. Sweat bathes her face. It is a young, sweet, calm face. Her husband lightly kisses her cheek.

The obstetrician slips into a sterile gown, which the nurse ties for him. Encouraging the patient, he examines her and tells her that the baby will be born with the next contraction.

"Stop pushing!" he says.

Through the mirror husband and wife watch the birth of their baby.

"It's a girl, Laura!"

The young mother cries out joyously. She and her husband embrace and in a few moments she is holding her daughter in her arms on the delivery table. The baby's tiny fist closes over her father's little finger. . . .

On the pediatric-service floor a twelve-year-old boy has just been admitted to the unit with a severe asthmatic attack. He is being treated with epinephrine injections and a nebulizer. The nurse stays with him and tries to keep him as calm as possible, while his mother waits nervously outside.

The phone at the nurses' station keeps ringing. A child in a sickle cell crisis is being admitted from the emergency room. Across the hall a spinal tap is going on—a possible case of meningitis. In a big room gaily decorated with storybook figures a teacher tutors three first-graders.

Two more children are coming down on stretchers from the recovery room. They will need the nurse's attention.

Over the loudspeaker another code is called. There has been a three-car collision on the West Side Highway. The transplant and bypass operations are still going on. All of the O.R.'s are busy. It is lunchtime and the aides and orderlies are getting ready to deliver the trays. The clinics are jammed. Patients have been waiting since early morning to be seen by their doctors. People are always waiting. Yet the life of the hospital goes on. It never stops. . . .

2.
The Lady with the Lamp

NURSING

Right now there are approximately 600,000 R.N.'s (registered nurses) active in their profession, and at least another 300,000 are needed to provide the health care required in the United States. Nursing offers a wide range of opportunities for personal growth and career advancement. As a profession it has changed radically since the 1950's. Going along with the trend for specialization, nursing has grown in complexity and sophistication. Today the nurse has the chance to develop his or her talents and skills in a chosen specialty. For example, R.N.'s are now superb C.C.U. and I.C.U. (intensive care unit) practitioners. In fact, they have become highly proficient clinicians in every area of medicine.

Both the coronary care and intensive care units of major hospitals have until recently been dominated by M.D.'s, but now the nurse has learned how to handle complex equipment—pacemakers, defibrillators, and monitors—which may determine life or death for the acutely ill patient.

Other nurses are trained midwives. Many hospitals have midwives on their staffs who do most of the uncomplicated deliveries. They are also found in rural areas, where physicians are scarce.

New programs designed to develop pediatric nurses have provided top-notch experts to take over some of the load of overworked pediatricians. The R.N. does all the preliminary patient interviewing and routine physical examination of the child. In cases where complications are apparent and beyond a nurse's scope, she calls upon the physician to take over.

In psychiatry, the nurse is moving into a meaningful role. In many hospitals with active community medical departments, the psychiatric nurse has the closest contact with the mental patient and his family, and works with the patient in group therapy. In fact, some psychiatrists have hired nurses to work for them as active therapists. Custodial care is a relic of the past.

Nurses everywhere are more alive, more vital, and are better trained than ever before. They are just beginning to realize their true potential.

In the hospital or the community, the R.N. is a leader with increased responsibility and an opportunity to advance. Regardless of your interests, there is a place for you on the health team in the specialty of your choice, provided you have the ambition and faith and enough drive to work hard.

Nursing services are desperately needed in both the city and the country. You can work in a hospital, in a public health agency, in industry, in a private office, or in the armed forces. The Army, Navy, and Air Force offer exciting professional and educational opportunities for nurses.

If nursing is your goal, you must first of all decide the type of study program. There are three routes you can take on the road to becoming an R.N.:

1. The two-year A.A. (Associate Arts) degree.
2. The three-year hospital-based diploma program.
3. The four-year baccalaureate course, leading to a B.S. (Bachelor of Science) degree. Some schools offer five-year programs.

All of these programs will enable you to take the licensing examination in your state. Credits from the diploma and A.A.-degree schools of nursing can be applied toward a Bachelor of Science degree if at any time an R.N. wants to continue her education.

There are twelve hundred nursing schools in the country and you must be sure that the school you choose is accredited by the A.N.A. (American Nurses Association) and the state board of nursing in your state. N.L.N.E. (National League for Nursing Education) accreditation is also most important. This is an organization devoted to maintaining the highest possible standards of nursing education. You can obtain from the League valuable information about accredited nursing schools throughout the United States, along with the latest facts about each program, including tuition costs. Many scholarships are available, and the school of your choice can supply additional information and resources to contact.

Suppose, though, that you decide it is impractical at the present time to take the two-, three-, or four-year nursing program. But you say you love nursing. Is there any option open to you?

You bet there is! And a very good one: licensed practical nursing. This is a flexible part- or full-time program that can be taken through a local high school, hospital, or other agency. Only one year of training is required to become a practical nurse.

Practical nurses are a vital adjunct to the hospital team of physicians, R.N.'s, and technicians, for they are most often at the patient's bedside whether in the hospital, home, or clinic. Furthermore, the practical nurse can always go back to college or nursing school to work for an R.N. and a degree.

THE URBAN PUBLIC HEALTH NURSE

"It's going to squeeze your arm for a minute."

Wearing slacks instead of a uniform, a student nurse checks a third-grader's blood pressure in the library of St. Francis de Sales School. Patiently, the boy's classmates wait their turn.

The innovator of this unique experiment in community medicine is a petite, twenty-one-year-old dynamo, Elizabeth Cintron. Elizabeth's parents fled Franco's Spain for Puerto Rico and finally came to the United States. Now Elizabeth is a third-year nursing student in the baccalaureate program of the City University of New York. Affiliated with Mount Sinai Hospital, the University has reached out to young people, including high school students, who perhaps have not dared to dream that college is real—that it is there if they want it.

Like Elizabeth, and her classmates, you can find personal satisfaction and a deep sense of accomplishment in a health career. The community needs you.

Community medicine, in which Elizabeth Cintron is involved, has changed the concept of medical care throughout the country. The Mount Sinai outreach program has successfully linked the hospital's medical services with the area it serves. At St. Francis de Sales, Elizabeth is funded by a grant. She has set up a health program to give medical checkups to the children. In such a program, liaison people, like dentists, provide whatever additional services are needed. A nutritionist counsels parents about their children's eating habits and plans special diets for the overweight and underweight students. An expert in physical fitness gives a class in exercise and body conditioning.

Elizabeth has established a warm relationship with the children and their parents. There is also—and most important—an ethnic bond between them. They know she cares, she understands; they trust her. So she is able to give the parents and their children the kind of counseling they need. She answers their questions and refers them to the hospital's clinics, being careful to provide instructions on how to seek the right type of service for their special problems.

Most people are terrified of the unknown. They want to know what to expect. The numerous clinics of a large, complex hospital can be staggering to someone standing in the entrance lobby. Elizabeth gives them confidence and supplies the information they need to find the right clinic.

When Elizabeth graduates, she plans to dedicate herself to this new and exciting field of community medicine. She wants to work with the inner-city people and bring health care to those who need it—where they need it.

If you are a high school student with aspirations like Elizabeth's, there are a great many careers open to you. The health field is wide open for anyone who wants the soul-satisfying experience of giving to and helping others. These careers are also well paying. Step by step, inch by inch, you can climb the ladder to the top in a highly respected profession. And there is help available to point you in the right direction.

Just write to your state education department or to the American Nurses Association, whose address is given at the end of this chapter, for information.

Thousands of young Puerto Rican students in New York, Philadelphia, and Chicago, have realized their ambitions through Aspira. Aspira is a dynamic organization, devoted to preserving and developing the Puerto Rican community. It has succeeded.

Through its well-organized program, Aspira has started clubs in New York City's high schools. Their objective is to involve both parents and children in education. The clubs, led by Aspira leaders, hold rap sessions with the students to instill self-confidence and discipline and to encourage good study habits and motivation. When a student falls behind in his schoolwork, they provide tutorial help.

When the student is ready, Aspira helps him plan his college education and define his career goals. A special unit helps with scholarship and loan assistance. While the student is in college he maintains a close link with his Aspira-mates, and he often takes an active role in helping other young Puerto Ricans along the same road.

If you are Puerto Rican, Aspira can give you the guidance you need to fulfill your ambitions. Other organizations, such as Breakthrough, are doing similar work in recruiting Black, Puerto Rican, and other minority students for careers in nursing. Breakthrough is a national organization with headquarters in New York. Both of these groups can be of great value to those who want both an education and a rewarding career.

Today hospital clinics are expanding into new types of home-care programs. Making home visits, nurses often notice the symptoms of a serious illness and alert the physician, who would otherwise be unaware of the patient's condition. Nurses have been used in cardiac projects involving the aged. They have through their expert home care actually lowered admissions to the hospital. The community stands to benefit greatly from the changing philosophy of hospital care, which has stimulated the development of community medicine and neighborhood health centers.

If you are a giving, warm, and compassionate person, then nursing, or one of the allied health careers, is what you are looking for. As it did for Elizabeth Cintron, nursing can provide you with many rewarding experiences. Elizabeth is out there in the streets of Manhattan's Upper East Side helping others. If you want to help too, there is a health career waiting for you. Many people are waiting for you. Don't let them wait too long.

For more information about nursing and the organizations that can answer your questions, write to the following:

>American Nurses Association
>10 Columbus Circle
>New York, New York   10019
>
>Aspira Educational Opportunity Center
>216 West 14th Street
>New York, New York   11201
>
>Aspira of New York, Inc.
>296 Fifth Avenue
>New York, New York   10001

Breakthrough
10 Columbus Circle
New York, New York   10019

National League for Nursing Education
10 Columbus Circle
New York, New York   10019

3.
Microbe Sleuths

In the hospital lab a technologist prepares a slide for the pathologist, who is waiting to study the cells under the microscope. The patient and the surgeon in the operating room wait too. Is it cancer?

Cytology is just one kind of laboratory work you can do as a medical technologist. Perhaps you are a detail-minded person, and you have liked mixing things in your mother's kitchen since you were a preschooler. You'd love the chem lab. You are also very dexterous with your hands. No bull in the china shop are you! Besides, you have that stick-to-itiveness quality essential for success in any field where things must be done right.

If this is a pretty good description of you, then you should consider becoming a certified laboratory technologist. You have four fields to choose from.

1. Certified laboratory assistant
2. Histology technician
3. Cytotechnologist
4. Medical technologist

The patient's life is held within the hands of the medical technologist and the other members of the lab team. Because of sophistication in technique and the ever-increasing work load, hospital labs have proliferated into special departments within the hospital. Their classification depends upon the kind of work in which they are involved. Even if you have never been in a hospital, most likely you have visited a doctor's office or clinic, where a nurse took a sample of your blood which was earmarked for "the lab." But which lab?

If the doctor wanted a complete blood count done, the specimen would be delivered to the hematology lab. The hematology lab in a hospital is a very busy place. It serves not only the inpatient areas, but outpatient facilities as well. Often reports are needed *stat* in emergencies. A patient can't go to the operating room until the surgeon has the report of his blood count, hematocrit value (ratio of red blood cells to volume of whole blood), W.B.C. (white blood cell count), and hemoglobin.

Technicians in the hematology lab do all of the blood counts and other tests, using special electronic equipment. These finely sensitive instruments enable the technician to determine precise, accurate cell counts. If the doctor has ordered a "differential," for example, the technician makes a stained smear so that the different kinds of cells present in the specimen can be determined. Other smears are taken from the bone marrow, where blood cells are formed, to see the types of cells being manufactured.

There are other tests, as well, which involve blood clotting. Sometimes the hematology lab is also called upon to take part in special tests concerning the diagnosis of rare diseases.

As a technician, regardless of where you work, you will not be isolated. There is much patient contact, as you are the person who takes the blood samples. Visiting the patient almost daily, you can develop a most meaningful rapport with him. He may open up to you. Perhaps he just needs a sympathetic person to talk to so he can unburden his anxieties about his illness, his concern for his family, for his future. The patient may bring up an extremely important problem which you can't handle but which the doctor, nurse, or social worker can solve. Thus, you would be in a position to get the right kind of help for the patient when he needs it.

The chemistry lab is another busy section, and it carries a heavy work load in any hospital. Here, innumerable tests are performed, many by technicians. And although various electronic devices are employed, the demand for qualified technicians is staggering.

As you can readily understand, the blood bank is a most important department in any hospital. Donors who give blood must be typed and cross-matched with excruciating care. A blood reaction from infusing a patient with the wrong blood can be fatal.

There is a great deal of pressure in the blood bank. The medical technologist has to handle the onus of reponsibility, and it is a challenging job when that phone rings and there is a call for several units of typed, cross-matched blood. However, it is a very exciting place to work. You can derive tremendous satisfaction from realizing how important your job is when that *stat* order comes in and you are doing the typing and cross-matching of a patient's blood. It's a time to pause a moment—and pray. Your integrity may save a patient's life.

What goes on in the cytology lab? As you have probably guessed from studying the word, it has to do with the study of cells, especially cancer cells. This is the domain of a highly skilled laboratory technician called a cytotechnologist. It is where cervical smears, "Pap" tests, are prepared which screen thousands of women every year for the presence of cancer. Many other smears are also performed from other body specimens to determine the presence of the cancer cell or its precursor.

The cytotechnologist who does discover abnormalities on a suspect smear refers it immediately to the pathologist for his expert evaluation. Diligence and accuracy are the most important characteristics of the cytotechnologist.

Next door, in histology, tissue studies are performed. The surgeon always sends the histology lab tissue specimens excised during surgery so that a slide can be prepared and examined by the pathologist. The histology technician learns to set up these slides, slicing the tissue into fine pieces, so that it can be studied microscopically. Also, the technician uses various dyes to reveal the structure of the cells.

Perhaps, on the other hand, you see yourself as another Louis Pasteur, fighting diseases as a super microbe sleuth! Then the place for you is the microbiology lab, where body excretions—blood, urine, and other substances—are examined for bacterial infestation. Identifying the causative agent in a disease is vital to determining the method of cure. Your role here would be very important.

The microtechnologist works with cultures and smears, plus a variety of bacterial organisms. Many new methods for shortening the time of bacterial identification are now being developed. In parasitology, the detective work involves searching for bacteria, parasitic ova, or other microscopic demons. Today people are traveling more than ever before, and rare microbes can be picked up under an African safari sun or on a trip down the Amazon. Working in a parasitology lab brings a whole new world into focus under the microscope. It is stimulating and challenging to the imagination, intellect, and powers of observation.

But how do you get into lab work? What kind of technician should you become? What are the educational requirements?

THE CERTIFIED LABORATORY ASSISTANT

Let us first consider the certified laboratory assistant. If you want to get into the field as quickly as possible and then further your education at a later date, consider a lab assistant's program. You will have to finish a four-year course at high school and graduate with a diploma and then train for twelve months at a hospital-based technology school for certified lab assistants. The school must have the sanction of the Board of Certified Laboratory Assistants of the American Society of Medical Technologists.

The course combines practical clinical experience with classroom work. After completing the program you must take an examination in order to earn the blue patch worn on your arm: C.L.A. As a certified laboratory assistant you can expect to earn between $5,000 and $8,000 a year to start, depending upon the area of the country in which you plan to work.

If this is your specialty, you should be a calm, well-organized person who loves detail work and can function under pressure. Bear in mind that any laboratory is an extremely active department and that many demands will be made upon you, whether you are collecting specimen samples or checking lab equipment.

The job of certified laboratory assistant is the first step on the ladder of health-career success. Once you have become proficient you can get additional training and work toward a medical technologist's career. In all probability the hospital you choose will have an on-the-job training program of which you can take advantage.

THE HISTOLOGY TECHNICIAN

If your main interest turns out to be working with tissues, then histologic technology is your field. Remember, as a histology technician, you are the one who prepares the slide that the pathologist, the Sherlock Holmes of the laboratory, searches for abnormalities. In your training program you will learn to slice tissues extremely thin. Also, you will be involved in staining the tissues with special dyes and in mounting them properly.

Like the laboratory assistant, you must take a year of training in a pathology lab after graduation from a four-year accredited high school program. The Board of Registry of Medical Technologists will grant certification if you pass the examination. As a histology technician you can earn approximately $5,000 to $10,000 a year to start.

THE CYTOTECHNOLOGIST

Beyond the one-year training programs, we get into the two-year college course which prepares you to be a cytotechnologist. During the two years you spend in college, you must take at least twelve hours of biology. The additional year of training that you will need in a cytotechnology school can be financed through scholarship funds. In fact, laboratory schools do not usually charge tuition, and many offer stipends to help you out during the training period. However, make sure your school has the

American Medical Association stamp of approval. Certification is granted by the Board of Registry of Medical Technologists when you pass the examination.

As a cytotechnologist, you will be concerned with the cells of the human body. Cancer is the disease your microscopic examination may pick up as you study those cell changes that often proliferate into cancer. Through your work, many early signs of cancer can be detected. Early treatment will usually save the patient's life. It is important to bear in mind that you will need all your resources of mental concentration and perseverance and a love of detail work to be successful in this field.

Cytotechnologists command salaries up to $11,000 a year. Besides at some future date, if you have the desire to do so, you can always return to college and complete the work required for the bachelor's degree. Then you can go on to medical technology.

THE MEDICAL TECHNOLOGIST

This is a step on the ladder just below the top man, the pathologist. As a medical technologist—if that should be your goal—your responsibility will be even greater than that of the laboratory assistant, histology assistant, or cytotechnologist.

It is you, the medical technologist, who will bear the excruciating pressure in the blood bank. You will be the one to study the blood of a mother who may be RH sensitized. You will stain the smear of a possibly virulent organism that is giving a patient a severe infection. You will check the amount of prothrombin (a blood-clotting agent) in the blood of a patient with a pulmonary embolism whose life hangs in the balance. You will find the elusive parasite confounding the medical men who don't know how to treat a certain patient. What antibiotic will work? You will give them the right answer when you nail those ova on the slide beneath the microscope. A child in the emergency room may have lead poisoning. It is you, the medical technologist, who will find the missing link and provide the doctor with the clue to a diagnosis that may save the child's life.

As in the other categories, you will receive financial assistance through the school's scholarship funds. The navy-blue-and-white patch of certification is yours when you pass the exam. It is a lucrative career; your income can soar to $13,000. It is a challenge. Exciting? Yes! Mentally stimulating? You bet! Join the ranks of a highly respected profession as an M.T.!

By the mid-1970's we will need an additional seventy thousand technologists. The field is changing rapidly. The future is computerization, and the lab will be automated as much as possible. A finer degree of competence will be needed to work with computerized equipment. Smaller labs will be absorbed into larger ones, so say the experts. Obviously, this will be of great benefit to the small towns and rural areas that lack hospitals. Rather than have many small hospital-based labs that cannot cope with the complexity of the tests that must be done, a large lab serving many towns is more feasible and more practical.

The demand for tests of every type will grow, and so will the work load in most labs. Many different kinds of workers will find themselves in a new and vital era of technology. You may experience many changes. There will be a need for computer-oriented people with this kind of training to work with highly sensitive instruments.

Many different specialists will be involved in this fast-developing field. Why not get in there now? Be there when the changes take place. Live and work in a field where your skills are most important.

For further information about careers in medical technology, contact the following:

    American Society for Microbiology
    1913 I Street, N.W.
    Washington, D.C. 20006

    Association of Schools of Allied
      Health Professions
    1 Dupont Circle
    Suite 300
    Washington, D.C. 20036

    American Association of Blood Banks
    Suite 1322
    30 North Michigan
    Chicago, Illinois 60602

    American Medical Association
    535 North Dearborn Street
    Chicago, Illinois 60610

    American Society of Clinical Pathologists
    2100 West Harrison Street
    Chicago, Illinois 60612

    American Medical Technologists
    710 Higgins Road
    Park Ridge, Illinois 60068

    Registry of Medical Technologists
    P.O. Box 2544
    Muncie, Indiana 47302

National Committee for Careers in
the Medical Laboratory
9650 Rockville Pike
Bethesda, Maryland 20014

National Institutes of Health
Bureau of Health Manpower Education
Information Office
9000 Rockville Pike
Bethesda, Maryland 20010

Foundation for Medical Technology
Mount Sinai Medical Center
11 East 100th Street
New York, New York 10029

American Society of Medical Technologists
Hermann Professional Building
Suite 25
Houston, Texas 77025

4.
The Breath of Life—
The Inhalation Therapist

Did you ever run up a hill so fast that you couldn't catch your breath? Remember how hard it was to breathe? There was a pain in your chest; your face felt hot and flushed. It was a terrifying feeling. Or perhaps you or a member of your family suffers from asthma.

Respiration is essential for life. An airway for breathing and adequate ventilation is the first thing a critically ill patient needs.

If this aspect of health care intrigues you, then consider studying to be an inhalation therapist. As such a therapist you would be an integral part of the medical team. It is a profession that requires a quick intelligence, a calm nature, and an ability to handle emergencies. The patient's life depends upon your sharp thinking and good judgment.

The inhalation therapist needs a sound background in science and a thorough understanding of how the breathing apparatus works. He must be aware of the way gases are interchanged in the lungs and be able to handle the equipment necessary in the treatment of patients with chest ailments.

What are the primary functions of the inhalation therapist? First of all, you will learn to assist the physician in C.P.R. (cardio-pulmonary resuscitation) and to handle the equipment properly. You will teach patients and other members of the health team how to use respirators, nebulizers, and other machines that help breathing.

A knowledge of temperature and the atmosphere is a must for an inhalation therapist. You have to understand how to use oxygen, and you must know how to control humidity. It will be your job to give oxygen and other gases through the nose with a nasal tube or by the use of a mask or tent, and it will be important to appreciate the right way to administer such gases as helium or carbon dioxide and to know the proper use of aerosol medications. You'll need to know physics principles, too, when it comes to working with new kinds of equipment in which positive pressure is necessary.

The therapist should also be capable of interpreting blood gas samples and should have a thorough knowledge of suction techniques.

As you can see, it is a job for the person who wants to learn a highly technical and valuable skill. After all, the patient's next breath will depend on you!

Interestingly enough, most of us take the act of breathing for granted. It's involuntary. So we are unconscious of what is going on inside our bodies. Nevertheless, we will die if the interchange of gases within the lungs is in any way obstructed.

Breathing is not a function separate from respiration, as many people think. It is closely related to respiration, for the action of the diaphragm and chest impels air into the lungs and out of them again.

Respiration is more complex. It involves not only the passage of air in and out of the pulmonary system, but also oxygenation. During respiration, oxygen is carried into the pulmonary blood vessels from the lungs. The

The Breath of Life—The Inhalation Therapist

blood transports it to every part of the body. The respiratory process synthesizes the use of oxygen and produces carbon dioxide in the body cells. Another important feature of respiration entails the movement of carbon dioxide from the blood to the lungs.

When we breathe in, our muscles contract and the diaphragm is lowered; thus the chest wall expands in an upward and forward motion. Obviously, this action increases the thoracic area. The lungs are elastic so they expand when the intrapleural pressure drops.

During normal breathing, we do not require muscle activity for exhalation. When the muscles used in inspiration relax again, the chest falls and the diaphragm resumes its normal position. Thus, the thoracic cage decreases in size, intrapleural pressure rises, and the lungs revert to their former state. The air passes out of the lungs because the intrapulmonary pressure exceeds the pressure of the atmosphere.

Every inhalation therapist must know the mechanism of respiration and understand the terminology. It is absolutely vital for the therapist to know the difference between intrapulmonary and intrapleural pressure because he or she is concerned with these differences. Intrapulmonary pressure refers to pressure within the lungs. Intrapleural pressure is pressure within the space between the lungs and the thoracic wall.

The study of respiration and the interchange of air and gases is a most complex one. During your course of study, as you work in the area of anatomy and physiology, you will learn these points in depth.

As an inhalation therapist your services will be in great demand. Think of the rapidly rising number of chronically ill and elderly patients with such chest ailments as emphysema, asthma, and cardiac dysfunction. Bear in mind also that all large city hospitals are doing more open-heart surgery than ever before.

Inhalation therapists are trained to cope with serious breathing and respiratory conditions that demand quick action. C.P.R. technique is a must for every therapist. When this code is called over the P.A. system in the hospital, you may be the first person to reach the critically ill patient. You may save his life with your knowledge of resuscitation techniques.

The inhalation therapist is the best-trained person to deal with respiratory emergencies, except, in the case of an arrest, when the anesthesiologist and corps of physicians direct all resuscitation methods.

The entire hospital, however, leans heavily on the inhalation therapist's services. He must be able to meet the needs of patients with respiration problems in every department. Some hospitals have special clinics devoted to treating such conditions as asthma or emphysema. In the future a home-care service may well be a part of the hospital's community medicine approach. Thus you would treat many patients at home rather than wait until they were forced to go to the hospital.

Teaching is of utmost importance. As an inhalation therapist you will be responsible for showing the patients how to use nebulizers correctly, for example. Patients also suffer from psychological fears, and your job will be to establish warm, sympathetic relationships with them. Remember, chest diseases can be extremely debilitating. They affect a person's entire life-style and make it hard for him to earn a living. The changes in his life will reflect themselves in anxiety and in depression over his condition.

The Breath of Life—The Inhalation Therapist

The therapist's role is multifaceted. He helps the patient face his illness, deal with it positively, and build a different, slower-paced kind of life. To do the job well, you will need intelligence, warmth, compassion, patience, understanding, and a high degree of manual dexterity.

There are job opportunities all over the country, especially in big cities. Don't forget, however, that a hospital operates on a twenty-four-hour-a-day basis, so you may be required to work in the evening or at night. In any health career you have to realize that people are sick all around the clock. A hospital can't close down at five thirty! The need must be met, and you will discover that the work is so rewarding you will be willing to make these sacrifices—not grudgingly, but with a real sense of caring.

As a therapist you will be called upon to care for both critically ill and chronic patients. But let's say you are the inhalation therapist on duty when the emergency room receives a patient with a severe chest injury. This is a trauma case. Rushing to the scene, you would first assess the patient's condition and secure an airway so that he could breathe. Of course the rest of the team would soon arrive, but the most important step for you would be to get the patient breathing—if at all possible. In some cases it might be too late, but all efforts must be extended to save a patient's life. It may be necessary to maintain the airway with the insertion of an endotracheal tube.

If a lung injury is apparent, the doctor would not want positive pressure applied, for that could cause a pneumothorax (collapsed lung). The only time you apply pressure is when you are using water-sealed chest drainage.

As you can see, the inhalation therapist must be prepared at any time for an acute emergency. He must know how to act quickly and expertly without a moment's hesitation. Naturally, not every case is an emergency, but any patient with breathing and respiratory difficulties has psychological problems and needs help and support through this difficult time. The therapist can supply positive empathic understanding.

From the technical point of view, the inhalation therapist must have the skill to evaluate a patient's condition. Obviously, you will use different methods in handling an acutely distressed patient and one who is chronically ill.

The department of inhalation therapy in any big-city hospital is very much a part of the scene and is necessary to every medical and surgical unit. If you think this is the specialty for you, consider the educational requirements. In high school you should take courses in biology, chemistry, and mathematics. After that, colleges and hospitals offer two-year programs that confer the A.A.S. (Associate in Applied Science) degree. Also, they prepare you for certification by the American Medical Association and the American Registry of Inhalation Therapists.

The course is a combination of classroom work and supervised clinical practice. Naturally, you will be most concerned with pulmonary diseases and chemistry, but the program also includes the intensive study of anatomy, pulmonary function, and physics.

To obtain certification as an inhalation therapist, it is important to choose a school whose program is accredited by the Technician Certification Board of the American Association for Inhalation Therapy.

As a registered therapist you can earn over $8,000 a year to start. Your salary will increase as the demand for qualified people rises.

The Breath of Life—The Inhalation Therapist

The following organizations can tell you the location of an accredited school in your state. Contact them for more information about this exciting career:

>Association of Schools of Allied
>   Health Professions
>1 Dupont Circle
>Suite 300
>Washington, D.C. 20036
>
>American Association for
>   Inhalation Therapy
>3554 Ninth Street
>Riverside, California 92501
>
>National Environmental Health Association
>1600 Pennsylvania Avenue
>Denver, Colorado 80203
>
>American Medical Association
>535 North Dearborn Street
>Chicago, Illinois 60610

For those who live in the New York area, here is a list of colleges and hospitals with accredited courses in inhalation therapy:

>Erie Community College
>Main and Youngs Road
>Williamsville
>Buffalo, New York 14225
>
>Borough of Manhattan Community College
>134 West 51st Street
>New York, New York 10020

New York University Medical Center
School of Inhalation Therapy
550 First Avenue
New York, New York 10016

Roosevelt Hospital
School of Respiratory Therapy
428 West 59th Street
New York, New York 10019

State University of New York
Upstate Medical Center
School of Health Related Professions
766 Irving Avenue
Syracuse, New York 13210

5.
Those Who Walk in Darkness

A young woman paces up and down the empty dayroom of a state mental hospital. Outside, on the tree-shaded lawn, other patients visit with relatives and friends. A band of sunlight slithers around the bars in the windows and hovers in a corner like a mute, depressed woman. No one has come to see Martha.

She twists a damp handkerchief between her fingers and breathes with a heavy sigh. Tears well up in her eyes. She thinks of her four children at home and wonders how they are managing.

What was wrong with her? Why couldn't she be like other women? She had everything—didn't she? A good husband, a beautiful home—well, a nice comfortable home—healthy children. And yet, the dead weight inside her made her feel as if she were sinking, sinking so deep within herself that one day she would disappear.

She was crazy. Only a crazy person thought of things like that. Distorted. Her view of herself and her life was distorted. Wasn't that what the psychiatrist said? That was why she was here. Why did her husband bring her to a mental hospital if she wasn't sick? They all said she was sick. Reactive depression. Involutional something-or-other. Words, words, words. She was tired. All she wanted was to be silent, to be still. . . .

"Martha."

She turned around. He was standing there, far away at the end of the hall, a tiny speck. Why did he look so small?

"Martha. It's me, Dan." The figure drew closer.

She turned to stone. She had wanted so much to see him, but now she wanted him to go away. If only the doctor had a pill to chase out all the devils inside her. Or, if he were really powerful, let him say, "Hold thy peace. Come out of her."

Dan was standing near her. He touched her face.

"Tell them to come out of me," she whispered. "The devils . . ."

He took her in his arms. The sun brightened the room for a moment and then went down behind the hills beyond the iron gate. . . .

THE MENTAL HEALTH TECHNICIAN

Many people like Martha suffer from the torment of mental illness. Some need to be hospitalized; others can be treated at home or in community mental health centers. The approach to the treatment of psychiatric disorders is undergoing vast changes. Emphasis now is on more direct forms of therapy rather than the Freudian type of psychoanalysis. To meet the exigencies of the enormous mental health problems confronting our society, a new kind of technician has evolved on the psychiatric perimeter: the mental health, or psychiatric, technician.

Patients used to be tagged with diagnostic labels based upon their clinical symptoms. Today the method of treating mentally ill people has become more realistic and humane with the establishment of "milieu therapy." This means that the hospital creates a homelike environment for the patient and involves staff members in his therapy. Patients take an active part in their daily regimen, do more meaningful tasks, and lead a more normal existence in close contact with nurses—and now, psychiatric technicians.

For example, psychiatric nurses are no longer performing custodial care. They take the initiative in group therapy and interview and counsel patients and their families. They also work as leading team members in community mental health programs.

Some psychiatrists employ nurses in their private practice to help ease their case loads. Such nurses do active therapy on a one-to-one basis and in groups. Obviously, there is a great need to fill the gaps in mental health care with additional personnel who can work closely with patients in the hospital and the community.

Today the role of neighborhood mental health centers is being emphasized. For example, in New Mexico, there is a comprehensive mental health facility that treats patients in the community on a twenty-four-hour basis. Provisions are made for inpatient and outpatient services. Rehabilitation is an active part of the program, linking the facilities of the center with the community to which the patient will return.

For emergencies they have an innovation called the Psychiatric Walk-In Clinic, operating at a number of medical centers. In an emotional crisis, the distressed person can walk in and get help at any time. Also, much new work is going on in the area of suicide prevention, with the emphasis on public education.

In Brooklyn the Maimonides Medical Center is making its nurses and other staff members active participants in neighborhood mental health centers that serve the entire community. The objective, of course, is to help people avoid long-term hospitalization.

The majority of mental health problems can be worked out by means of short-term therapy with a team of sympathetic and sensitive professionals—doctors, nurses, social workers, and therapists—all working together for the benefit of the patient. Nearly everyone has some kind of emotional problem at some time during his lifetime that requires outside help. The neighborhood mental health center can provide this help.

What are some of the things that you—as a mental health assistant or technician—would do in a mental health center? First of all, you would be the first person the patient would meet on his admission to the hospital, because you would do the initial interview. You would also talk with the patient's family and, in this way, get a firsthand picture of the immediate problems. As a mental health technician, you would also learn to give certain psychological tests. Observing the patient's behavior and reactions would be an important part of the job.

In other words, the technician spends almost all of his time with the patient on a one-to-one basis. He can build an effective relationship with the patient and give him insight into his difficulties in adjusting to society.

There is a great demand for mental health workers in rural areas, which are usually lacking in trained medical personnel. Many progressive treatment centers have been developed—and are flourishing—in New Mexico, California, Texas, and Colorado. In the East exciting work is going on around the Boston area and in New York City. There will, of course, always be a great need for additional people in the big-city poverty pockets, where the problems are extremely complex because they involve socioeconomic conditions as well. But the outlying areas of the country are equally hungry for help—all they can get. The opportunities are endless.

A mental health technician must be a very special kind of person, someone who has great personal insight. Are you that kind of person? What makes you tick? What are your strengths and weaknesses? What turns you on or off? Just how honest can you be in facing yourself?

It is difficult for anyone to be willing—simply willing—to take that first step and really look into his inner being with a calm, objective, frank attitude. But you can't help another person if you are not fully aware of your own inner self.

You have to put yourself in the other person's skin—to see things, to feel, to live life as he does, in order to know him. At the same time you must never lose your own grip on reality or let down your standards. This entails a high degree of emotional maturity. A keen mind, empathy, patience, and tolerance for behavior that may be very different from yours and your friends are also indispensable qualities for a first-rate mental health technician. Mentally ill people are extremely sensitive. They sense how others feel about them. They can't be fooled. They know if someone is truly sincere and wants to help them.

A career in mental health is demanding. You will be called upon to give a great deal of yourself. But there is tremendous satisfaction to be gained from helping "those who walk in darkness." They need you to lead them into the light.

Do you think this is your kind of work? You will be

warmly welcomed if you decide to go into it. To become a mental health technician, as with all health careers, you must be a high school graduate. The next step is to apply to an accredited college for its program in mental health. The course takes two years and leads to the A.A.S. degree.

The courses include community mental health, biology, psychology, English, art, and music. You also study rehabilitation and take part in an internship program where you work in your field at a community agency or hospital. There are job opportunities everywhere. The government is funding many new mental health projects and is just waiting for people like you to fill positions in them. You may want to work with inpatients in a hospital. Or perhaps you prefer community medicine, a neighborhood mental health center, a clinic, or a special school for the mentally retarded or emotionally disturbed child. If you are a big-city person, you may gravitate to these areas.

On the other hand, if you have a yen to travel or consider yourself a country cousin, then you should explore the rural frontiers. The variety of available jobs is enormous for anyone with ambition, compassion, and ability.

California has been seeking professional status for mental health technicians and is upgrading the quality of their education and performance. As a result, the California Society of Psychiatric Technicians has helped develop a national group called the National Association of Psychiatric Technicians. In any California mental hospital a large proportion of the staff is composed of psychiatric technicians.

As a mental health technician you can earn approximately $7,000 a year to start. Increments and higher salaries are based on experience and education.

THE PSYCHIATRIC SOCIAL WORKER

Going beyond the scope of the mental health technician and the psychiatric nurse, you may find the field so interesting that you will decide to forge ahead with a career as a psychiatric social worker.

The psychiatric social worker is a very important part of the mental health team. His or her functions involve helping the patient go back over his life from childhood to the present and correlating all the pieces. Through a step-by-step process, which includes extensive interviews with all of the family members, the psychiatric social worker gains incisive insight into the patient's way of relating to others. The information learned about his background, life experiences, education, and early childhood will give the physician clues to the source of his illness and provide the psychiatrist with an invaluable tool in directing the patient's therapy. Without the psychiatric social worker, this would be a most difficult and time-consuming task.

One of the major aspects of the psychiatric social worker's function is to work effectively with the patient's family. Most families are hard hit when mental illness strikes and find it extremely difficult to face and cope with such a crisis; it affects everyone in the family.

The psychiatric social worker is in an excellent position to help the family understand the dynamics of the situation in order for them to change their patterns of behavior. Harmony is the goal. So by extending yourself and using your education and skills you, the psychiatric social worker, can help the family overcome conflicting feelings of guilt and hostility that may be directed toward the patient.

Thus, whether you work in a mental health center, clinic, or hospital, you would serve as a liaison between the patient and his family and the mental health team, coordinating the functions of the psychiatrist, the nurse, and the technician. You would also serve as an intermediary between the patient and his family, helping to create a positive therapeutic atmosphere in the home, so that the patient will be able to make a satisfactory transition from hospital to community upon his discharge.

Extremely knowledgeable in the availability of community resources, psychiatric social workers know whom to contact and when. They are experts in financial assistance and rehabilitation services. They give the family important information on how to utilize the agencies in their community.

Psychiatric social workers have many job opportunities open to them. They can work in hospitals, in mental health clinics, in schools, in rehabilitation agencies, and in public health and visiting nurse agencies. Many workers go into the armed services or the Veterans Administration, or they choose to teach. Some prefer the field of research.

Unlike the other health careers discussed, the psychiatric social worker needs considerably more education and training. However, if this field is what you are ultimately aiming for, you can begin on the first step of the ladder as a psychiatric technician and later on continue your education until you earn a bachelor's degree. Psychiatric social workers must study beyond the baccalaureate and work toward a master's degree in a program accredited by the Council on Social Work Education.

This is a worthwhile goal to aim for if you find you want to work with the mentally ill. As a psychiatric social worker you can earn up to $15,000 a year, and you will have a chance to grow professionally.

The field of mental health encompasses many disciplines. There is a great need for all kinds of workers trained on every level of patient-centered milieu therapy. The psychiatrist, psychiatric nurse, psychiatric technician, and social worker combine efforts as a team to help the patient in his own setting. Today psychiatry is very much aware of the impact our present social scene has upon the individual who takes flight from life's pressures. New ideas are being tried, not only in the United States, but also in England and Italy. These last two countries are experimenting with radical methods of combating mental illness. Their aim is to eliminate the socioeconomic barriers which the doctors in these programs feel are the cause of creating alienated, frustrated, lost, and lonely people. The results of their efforts should be interesting, once their impact has been evaluated.

The wall between the mentally ill patient and society is being stripped away. The future is exciting—and it is yours.

For additional information, contact the following:

>California Society of
> Psychiatric Technicians
>1127 Eleventh Street
>Sacramento, California   95814

>Council on Social Work Education
>345 East Forty-Sixth Street
>New York, New York   10017

>American Psychiatric Association
>1700 Eighteenth Street, N.W.
>Washington, D.C.   20009

American Psychological Association
1200 Seventeenth Street, N.W.
Washington, D.C. 20036

National Institutes of Health
Bureau of Health Manpower Education
Information Office
9000 Rockville Pike
Bethesda, Maryland 20014

American Social Health Association
1740 Broadway
New York, New York 10019

National Commission for Social Work Careers
2 Park Avenue
New York, New York 10016

National Association for Retarded Children
2709 Avenue E, East
Arlington, Texas 76112

National Association for Mental Health
1800 North Kent Street
Rosslyn, Virginia 22209

6.
The Rehab Corps

A most important group of health careers is listed under rehabilitation. These specialties are concerned with the task of helping the disabled patient return to a meaningful life, where he can function with as much independence as possible.

Have you ever known someone who was recovering from a stroke? Or seen a child with a cleft palate who had a severe speech impediment? Do you know a Vietnam War veteran paralyzed from the waist down? Rehabilitation people are experts at dealing with such problems and at helping the crippled learn to walk and move and speak again. There are few satisfactions greater in life than using your know-how to enable the handicapped person to live a useful life once more.

THE PHYSICAL THERAPIST

Physical therapists are very much in demand. They need a high degree of dedication to minister to the paralyzed or to the crippled victims of illness and accidents.

As a therapist, your work will involve exercising immobile limbs, massaging, and utilizing the equipment found in hospital rehab units. You will have to learn about the body's muscles and how they work, so physiology is an important subject for you to take, along with courses in the behavioral sciences.

As a physical therapist you will spend a great deal of time teaching patients to walk again or how to use artificial limbs. Therefore you must be skilled in assessing the extent of the patient's disability so you can plan the right rehabilitation program for him. This is a long, often arduous task. The patient may become discouraged and depressed, particularly if he has led an active, independent life before his illness, and a person's mental state can greatly affect his recovery. Thus it is important for the therapist to encourage as much independent movement from the patient as possible. Many disabled people tend to regress. They can become childish and demanding because they discover that their illness gets them a great deal of attention from their families. Others nurture resentment and bitterness. Despairing, they ask the eternal, unanswerable question: "Why me, God? What did I do? Why?"

In these situations, spiritual counseling and psychological help are of great benefit, and it is up to the therapist to recommend such resources when they are indicated.

As soon as a disabled person begins an active therapy program, the therapist must instill confidence in him. If the patient has faith in his therapist, he will have more personal initiative and will want to work hard so that he can walk again or use his hands. Many special devices, particularly those used in veterans' hospitals, help the patient develop whatever physical function he has left in his affected muscles. When the patient is discharged from the hospital, he will need these self-help aids so that he can get along in the community within the limits of his disability.

Right now we could use more than fifty thousand physical therapists! With a $14,000-a-year earning power, it is a career to contemplate most seriously. If you have a scientific mind and manual dexterity, you might consider taking the four-year baccalaureate program necessary to become a physical therapist. It is well worth the investment. As with most health careers, you can get financial aid through scholarships and loans. The courses emphasized are chemistry, anatomy, physiology, psychology, and other sciences. A clinical internship is required to provide the necessary experience in physical therapy under supervision.

An accredited program leads to licensure, after passing the qualifying examination in the state where you are planning to practice. Write for additional information to:

> American Physical Therapy Association
> 1156 Fifteenth Street, N.W.
> Washington, D.C. 20008
>
> American Rehabilitation Counseling Association
> 1607 New Hampshire Avenue, N.W.
> Washington, D.C. 20009
>
> Registry of Medical Rehabilitation
>   Therapists and Specialists
> 4975 Judy Lynn
> Memphis, Tennessee 38118
>
> National Rehabilitation Counseling Association
> 1522 K Street, N.W.
> Washington, D.C. 20005

However, if you are unable to spend four years in college but are still interested in physical therapy, you can become a physical therapy assistant. Working under the supervision of the physical therapist, you would treat disabled patients with massage and exercise. Your role would be extremely important. And with this background you could always return to college at a future date and finish the four-year physical therapist's course.

There are many programs leading to the A.A.S. degree attached to universities and community colleges. The program for physical therapy assistants is two years in length, and although they are not licensed at the present time, some states are contemplating this step.

The program offers an opportunity to work with top-level professionals in hospitals and clinics, where there is always something interesting to be learned and explored as you perfect the skills that may help a disabled man or woman to walk again. Because of the work physical therapists and their assistants are doing, these patients are no longer ignored as "hopeless cripples."

The organizations listed for physical therapists can answer your questions also and provide helpful information about physical therapy assistant's programs.

THE SPEECH THERAPIST

One of the most intriguing areas for the dedicated health pro is a career in speech therapy. Have you ever wondered what it would be like to lose your voice? Can you imagine what it must have been like for the movie actress Patricia Neal when, after her massive stroke, she discovered that she knew what she wanted to say, but could not speak?

The speech therapist is a unique person. Often former theatrical people become interested in speech therapy because of their superior training in speech during their acting careers. It takes an individual with rare creative talents to be successful in this demanding field, which requires patience, diligence, emotional stability, and a sense of humor. In particular, the speech therapist who works with children should be a warm person who can make a child smile and laugh. Nowhere is this more important than with victims of a cleft palate. Many big medical centers have special clinics set up to handle palate problems exclusively.

The speech pathologist-therapist can practice privately or in a hospital, and may deal with one type of disorder or many combined problems. Some therapists, for example, are experts in aphasia, which means that, like Miss Neal, the afflicted person can think of a word but is unable to form it. This happens frequently to stroke victims. It takes long, hard, patient work to teach such a person to speak again.

Where facial and dental problems complicate a patient's speech disorder, the therapist makes recommendations to the dentist about the best type of prosthetic device for him.

The speech therapist has a complex job, and obviously, this kind of work requires considerable schooling: first, graduation from a baccalaureate program, then graduate school and the master's degree. Many speech therapists go farther and obtain the Doctor of Education degree, which gives them the opportunity to become heads of their departments and to earn up to $20,000 a year.

There are many excellent programs if you are interested. The period of study is long, but if it is what you want, go to it! It can be done if you have the discipline and the drive to succeed.

If you are drawn to this fascinating field, write to the following for more information:

American Speech and Hearing Association
9030 Old Georgetown Road
Bethesda, Maryland 20014

State University of New York at Albany
College of Arts and Sciences
Albany, New York 12203

State University of New York at Buffalo
University Center at Buffalo
Buffalo, New York 14214

Queens College
Department of Communication
Arts and Sciences
Flushing, New York 11367

Adelphi University
Speech and Hearing Program
Garden City, L.I., New York 11530

Ithaca College
Ithaca, New York 14850

Columbia University
Teachers College,
525 West 120th Street
New York, New York 10027

Graduate Program in Speech, Hearing Sciences,
    Speech Pathology, and Audiology
Graduate School and University Center
    of the City University of New York
33 West 42nd Street
New York, New York 10036

New York University
School of Education
80 Washington Square
New York, New York 10003

Syracuse University
Division of Speech Education
Syracuse, New York 13210

THE OCCUPATIONAL THERAPIST

Let's suppose you are a very artistic person. What career will usefully combine creative ability and practical experience? The occupational therapist, of course.

Accomplishing a task successfully sometimes does more for a patient's morale than any other kind of therapy. Creating something useful or beautiful can restore a person's self-esteem. To make this possible, the occupational therapist uses his or her skill and artistic capacities to teach the long-term patient how to work with his hands.

Most hospitals have an occupational therapy department. Mental hospitals and mental health clinics rely on it. To be this kind of therapist you need a warm personality as well as creative ability and much patience. It takes time and understanding to teach the elderly, for example, how to crochet or knit or sew, or perhaps how to work with leather or wood. The therapist must exercise good judgment in evaluating the patient's disability so as to develop his skills within the scope of his limitations.

So, if you have the imagination, the artistic talent, and a willingness to serve, here is a good way to do it—as a trained O.T. You may have seen occupational therapists at work in a hospital. Note they wear an O.T.R. (occupational therapy rehabilitation) patch on their white coats.

Occupational therapy requires a four-year college course leading to the bachelor's degree. Besides classroom work, supervised clinical experience is a major part of the program.

The American Occupational Therapy Association gives an examination that the therapist must pass to be registered. To learn more about this fascinating field, write to:

National Association for Music Therapy
P. O. Box 610
Lawrence, Kansas 66044

American Art Therapy Association
Menninger Foundation
Topeka, Kansas 66601

American Occupational Therapy Association
251 Park Avenue South
New York, New York 10010

As in physical therapy, there is also an occupational therapy assistant's program for those who cannot spend four years in college. Acting under the aegis of the professional occupational therapist, the trained assistants work with the disabled and chronically ill. The need for occupational therapy is great, and this category on the health career ladder is a most valuable one. The assistant therapist teaches aged people to sew, knit, and crochet. Both men and women enjoy the satisfaction of painting or working with clay. Just bringing a smile to a handicapped elderly person, perhaps one who is bedridden, is a job well done. You can do it with a compassionate heart and the skills you will learn as an occupational therapy assistant.

The program calls for two years of college, an A.A.S.-degree course that gives the student eligibility for certification by the American Occupational Therapy Association. You can apply these two years for credit in a bachelor's degree program if you decide to continue your education.

Occupational therapists earn between $6,000 and $9,000 a year or more; assistants make from $5,000 to $7,000. There are thousands of disabled people lying

The Rehab Corps

alone in hospital rooms, feeling lost and forgotten. They need someone young to teach them "how to do something." Reach out. Give to those who need you and it will come back to you many times over.

THE RECREATION THERAPIST

If you happen to have a wide range of interests and are a good organizer as well, an excellent career choice for you is that of the recreation therapist. Recreation therapists are essential to the long-term patient's recovery, particularly those who are in mental hospitals. These experts organize social events and arrange parties, picnics, dramatic presentations, athletic and bridge games, and trips to town to the art galleries or museums. The purpose of the recreation therapist's role is to stimulate social interaction among those who are mentally ill. The physical activities also give the patients a sense of vigor and well-being, and draw them into situations where they can relate to one another.

Nursing homes, too, are places that can benefit from the addition of a recreation therapist to the staff. The aged and chronically ill need to be taken out of themselves. The therapist provides suitable outlets for them appropriate to their condition. Most elderly people enjoy card parties, musical events, and movies. Diversions of this nature can do wonders for their morale.

The recreation therapist needs an outgoing, friendly personality. It is a great career for a "doer." To become a recreation therapist you also need four years of college and a bachelor's degree. It is important that you participate in extracurricular activities in school and are versatile in such areas as music, art, and dance. An interest in sports is also advisable.

You may instead elect to take a two-year course for an A.A.S. degree and work as a recreational therapy assistant. For either career more information can be obtained from:

>Consulting Service on Recreation for the
> Ill and Handicapped
>1700 Pennsylvania Avenue N.W.
>Washington, D.C. 20006
>
>National Recreation and Park Association
>1700 Pennsylvania Avenue, N.W.
>Washington, D.C. 20006
>
>National Therapeutic Recreation Society
>1700 Pennsylvania Avenue, N.W.
>Washington, D.C. 20006

7.
The Rest of the Team

THE X-RAY TECHNICIAN

A patient is wheeled into the X-ray department. The room is equipped with machines capable of scanning the entire body. At that point the X-ray technician, or radiologic technologist, enters the scene. A most important person, the X-ray technician gets the patient ready for a variety of radiologic examinations, prepares and takes X rays, and makes sure that safety precautions are rigidly enforced. The technician works under the direct supervision of the radiologist, a physician trained to read X rays with expert precision.

The X-ray technician must understand the complicated equipment he uses every day and be able to handle these high-voltage machines safely and efficiently.

Other highly specialized technicians, whose jobs require additional education, deal with the treatment of cancer and related diseases, and work with cobalt, radium, and radioactive isotopes.

Those who are involved with the latter are called nuclear-medicine technologists. The nuclear technologist works very closely with the physician and helps him in the use of isotopes. He becomes an expert in utilizing the complex machines that are concerned with tracer studies of radioactive substances injected into the body.

This is a well-paying field, and the career is a solid one in which you can combine technical skills with extensive patient contact. There is always something new to be learned in radiologic technology.

To be licensed as an L.R.T. (laboratory radiologic technician), you must take a two-year course and pass the examination. Then you can be certified by the American Registry of Radiologic Technicians. You can find out more about a career as an X-ray technologist by writing to the following organizations for information:

> American Society of Radiologic Technologists
> 645 North Michigan Avenue
> Chicago, Illinois 60611
>
> Society of Nuclear Medical Technologists
> 1201 Waukegan Road
> Glenview, Illinois 60025

THE DIETITIAN

After the patient returns to his room from the X-ray department, he may be extremely hungry. Here's where the dietary department takes over and we meet the dietitian, another important person.

Perhaps the patient is a cardiac case or is hypertensive, and needs a special diet. A person faced with a sudden change in his eating habits requires a sympathetic, knowledgeable teacher to show him how to prepare his food properly and to tell him what to avoid.

The patient's condition is studied by the physician, who orders the diet. Then the dietitian prepares it, bearing in mind any food preferences the patient may have. The dietitian must be an expert in nutrition, and the

The Rest of the Team

hospital dietitian has the responsible position of supervising the preparation and serving of thousands of meals every day, as well as teaching patients and nursing students the basic principles of good nutrition in disease and health. It is a role that combines a knowledge of science with the desire to do something for others.

Dietitians must take a four-year baccalaureate program with a major in nutrition. It is also important to have an aptitude for chemistry and science. The American Dietetic Association requires a six- to twelve-month internship if the student wants professional status. Students must also include clinical experience in their course of study. Many dietitians go on to graduate school so they can go into research.

An experienced dietitian can expect a salary of from $15,000 to $20,000 a year. If food is your pleasure and you also have a scientific mind, perhaps the thought of becoming a dietitian will tickle your palate! If it does, write to:

> American Home Economic Association
> 2010 Massachusetts Avenue, N.W.
> Washington, D.C. 20036
>
> American Dietetic Association
> 620 North Michigan Avenue
> Chicago, Illinois 60611
>
> Institute of Food Technologists
> 211 North La Salle Street
> Suite 2120
> Chicago, Illinois 60601

If you are interested in nutrition but want to tackle the shorter route first, you can enroll in a two-year course leading to the dietitian assistant's position. This is the person who assists the dietitian in meal planning and who makes the diet tray attractive, tasty, and zesty. Dietitian assistants keep records, figure out caloric intake, and visit the patients to find out their food preferences. They try, whenever possible, to meet a patient's requests, as long as it conforms to his dietary regimen. Of course, when he asks for lobster, they smile sweetly and offer an alternative—sole or flounder.

Dietetic technicians earn up to $10,000 a year after completing a two-year A.A.S.-degree program. Pepper your high school program with generous amounts of home economics, science, and cooking, if you want to be a dietetic assistant.

THE DENTAL HYGIENIST

Another familiar person on the medical scene is the dental hygienist, the girl in white with the flashing, healthy TV smile! As a nation we are—and should be—concerned with teeth and oral hygiene. Many dentists employ hygienists, usually women, in their offices. They are trained to teach patients how to take care of their teeth and gums. The dentist who specializes in gum care makes the initial evaluation and plans the treatment, and the hygienist teaches the patient how to brush his teeth properly. She also assists the dentist in many office procedures. She removes stains and tartar from patients' teeth, cleans and polishes them, performs gum massage, and teaches the patient everything he should know about the care of his teeth. In addition, she takes X-rays of the mouth.

Often it is the dental hygienist who sets the tone between the patient and the dentist. If she establishes a good rapport with him, he will respond positively and realize the importance of daily mouth care. In many cases the teeth should be brushed and the gums massaged two or three times a day. Unless this type of routine is followed, chances are the patient will lose his teeth at an early age because of gum disease.

Hygienists earn approximately $8,000 a year. Many work in hospitals, but the majority are in dentists' offices. To become a dental hygienist, it is necessary to take a two-year A.A.S.-degree program at a university or college. If you have a movie-star smile, this may be the career for you. If so, flash that smile in the direction of:

American Dental Hygienists Association
211 East Chicago Avenue
Chicago, Illinois 60611

THE MEDICAL RECORD TECHNICIAN

With all those health pros involved in caring for hospital patients, someone has to keep the record straight. That job belongs to the medical record technician.

Records are essential for both medical and legal purposes, and correct charting of the patient's hospital stay is a must if the hospital is to have information about this illness. It will be your job to make sure the patient's chart has been accurately recorded, and you may even help the doctor make reports by gathering the necessary chart information. These charts, which are a source of research material for students, administrators, and physicians, will soon be available on miniature film and tape.

The M.R.T. also helps the medical record librarian and analyzes health data.

Many schools now offer A.A.S.-degree courses that are comprehensive in scope and give fascinating insight into the area of medical health records. For example, students study X-ray reports, pathology reports, and social service records, and, most important, they learn medical terminology. If you have a researcher's fact-finding mind, this is the career for you, and since work in this field will soon involve computers on a large scale, the ability to assess such data will be important. You should also have a liking for details.

In some hospitals you can get on-the-job training by taking a year's course in medical record technology; however, most technicians-to-be are enrolled in two-year A.A.S. programs, which are available at many community colleges.

As a medical record technician you can earn up to $6,000 a year—more if you decide to complete your education with an additional two years of college training and get your bachelor's degree. Then you can reach the top of your profession as a supervisor, where you will earn more money and have increased responsibility.

If this triggers your computer brain, contact:

>American Association of Medical
>   Record Technicians
>211 East Chicago Avenue
>Chicago, Illinois   60611

THE EMERGENCY ROOM TECHNICIAN

Do you recall the action in the emergency room? You

The Rest of the Team

can get into it as an M.E.T. (medical emergency technician), an emergency room technician. You are there when the patient is brought into the hospital after an accident. In fact, the M.E.T. is the first person the patient meets.

Only cool-headed pros belong in the E.R. You have to be calm to handle the many emergencies that occur day and night. But it's an exciting place to work. The M.E.T. learns how to handle every possible emergency and the use of emergency equipment.

The course takes two years and will give you an A.A.S. degree. They will be two years of intensive training. You will learn how to deal with injuries, what to do if a patient has been stabbed or shot, and how to bandage limbs or splint fractures. It is a fast-paced, intense, and comprehensive course for quick-thinking activists who want the excitement of working at top speed and at top pressure in one of the most dramatic areas of the hospital, the emergency room.

As a technician you will also learn C.P.R. (cardiopulmonary resuscitation) technique, because you must be prepared to face emergencies, and in many cases C.P.R. saves lives. Here, minutes count. There isn't time for any hesitation when a patient is brought into the E.R, in shock or cardiac arrest. Often the M.E.T. is the first person to receive a patient with a crushed chest. You have to know what to do. Of course, most hospital emergency rooms, with the exception of rural outposts, are staffed with competent physicians. Even so, you will be called upon to assist the doctor, and you must act fast.

It is an exciting assignment—an opportunity to use many needed skills. You can work in a hospital emergency room where medical emergency technicians are employed, or ride an ambulance as an attendant. Some big-city hospitals have teams that go directly to the scene of an emergency, rather than waiting for the patient to be brought to the hospital. This saves time and lives.

M.E.T.'s earn $7,000 a year to start, but as they gain experience and become seasoned pros, their income is upgraded to $10,000. To be a certified technician you must have Red Cross first-aid training and must have passed the Red Cross examination. Then you can take the two-year program, which includes supervised clinical experience.

States differ in their requirements. In New York, for example, there are special conditions governing the certification of medical emergency technicians. So you should check with your state to find out about its laws covering M.E.T. standards.

THE OPERATING ROOM TECHNICIAN

Another area of the hospital that offers the same kind of drama and excitement as the emergency room is the operating room. If you enjoy working under pressure and want to be part of a surgical team, you will want to know more about the career of operating room technician. This technician sets up the operating room for operations and passes instruments to the surgeon. It is a job that requires a great deal of dexterity and skill. R.N.'s once performed this function, but with the nursing shortage and the great demand for skilled personnel, the job of operating room technician came into being.

Working under the supervision of the R.N., the operating room technician learns the job right in the hospital O.R. Programs vary from nine months to one year. You can also take a two-year course at a community college. The course must have the approval of the Association of Operating Room Technicians. After graduation, the student is eligible to take the certification examination.

Contact your local hospital for more information about this health career opportunity. The salary is comparable to related health openings and will depend upon the area of the country in which you are working. As an O.R. technician, you can make a meaningful contribution to the surgical team.

For more information about careers as M.E.T.'s and O.R. technicians, write to the following:

> Association of Operating Room Technicians
> Denver Technological Center
> 8085 East Prentice Avenue
> Englewood, Colorado 80110

> Association of Schools of
>   Allied Health Professions
> 1 Dupont Circle
> Suite 300
> Washington, D.C. 20036

> American Medical Association
> 535 North Dearborn Street
> Chicago, Illinois 60610

8.
Climbing Up the Medical Ladder

Beyond the progressive, step-by-step health career ladder are those professions requiring more concentrated medical training. They offer the bright, conscientious, and intelligent young person a chance to carve an important place for himself in the nation's future.

In many instances, high school students whose aspirations have been bitterly thwarted because of socioeconomic disadvantages do not even dare to dream or hope that college or graduate school is possible for them. To be a dentist or a doctor is a difficult goal even for the son or daughter of a businessman or lawyer. How much more so for the less affluent, who have never met a doctor or dentist socially. How could they know what these men are like or what they do?

However, the dream can be anyone's who really has the motivation, intelligence, and discipline. Financial assistance is available, and so is help from many sources that are willing to give you encouragement, practical advice, and tutorial assistance when you need it.

THE OPTOMETRIST

A profession with vision in which you will find many rewards is optometry. Have you ever thought what it would be like if you could not see? It is indeed a terrifying idea. Yet most of us take this sensory organ for granted. We abuse our eyes, neglect visual problems, and fail to follow the advice of experts concerning eye care. Some people who need glasses rarely wear them. Most people ignore minor symptoms. But if eye problems are discovered early, simple corrections usually can be made that will prevent trouble later on. How easy it is to wear glasses or contact lenses or to perform eye exercises!

The person trained in this area, who is a most welcome member of the health team, is the optometrist. He is a skilled professional who can help you save your eyesight.

Have you ever wondered about the mechanism of vision? How do we see? What kind of miracle is it to be able to see? Anyone who works with cameras will easily understand visual principles, because our eyes operate in much the same way as a camera. The lens of a camera focuses the image on film. The lens of the eye does the same thing, except that the image is focused upon the retina, which is a group of nerve cells situated behind the eyeball. The iris, analogous to the camera's diaphragm, sharpens the image by controlling the light coming into the lens. Then inversion of the image occurs both in the human eye and the camera. The cortex of the brain reverses this "upside-down vision"; otherwise, we would see things upside down! What an amazing physiological process!

Many other complex actions are involved in the process of seeing, and it is interesting to pause and think about it a little. It gives us an appreciation not only of our own eyes, but also of the importance of protecting vision through good eye care. This is another important aspect of the optometrist's work.

The optometrist knows how to perform a thorough eye

examination with special instruments. Often he is the first person to pick up a local eye infection or even a serious disease in another part of the body, whose effects are observed in the eye. He may refer the patient to a physician if he suspects the patient has hypertension or diabetes. The optometrist corrects certain visual abnormalities in a patient by prescribing glasses or contact lenses, and he is skilled at fitting contact lenses, a task that requires considerable experience.

Optometrists command incomes of more than $20,000 a year in private practice. Six years of college and graduate work are required to become an O.D., or Doctor of Optometry. In the undergraduate program, the courses include math, chemistry, biology, and physics. During the four-year O.D. program, the student takes specialized courses in optics, pathology, math, optometric theory, and additional subjects. After graduation, he—or she, for optometry is now opening up to women—is qualified to take the licensure examination in his state. For further information contact these helpful organizations:

>American Optometric Association
>7000 Chippewa Street
>St. Louis, Missouri   63119

>State University of New York
>College of Optometry
>122 East 25th Street
>New York, New York   10010

>Ohio State University
>College of Optometry
>338 West Tenth Avenue
>Columbus, Ohio   43210

THE DENTIST

Dentistry is another highly lucrative and interesting career to consider. The need for qualified professionals in oral health care is staggering. Dentists easily find opportunities in private practice or in affiliation with hospital medical centers. They can specialize in oral surgery, orthodontia, or periodontia (which deals with gum care). Gum problems often account for the early loss of teeth, which in this country is fast becoming a major health problem. Dentists trained in this specialty perform an extremely important service by stressing prophylactic mouth care. They earn over $30,000 a year.

As our population grows, the need for expanded dental services rises. Children require early and careful treatment to protect their teeth from injury or disease, and the middle-aged also have problems requiring expert dental skill. Most dentists operate on an extremely busy schedule, often exceeding forty-five or fifty hours a week!

To begin the career path leading to the D.D.S. (Doctor of Dental Surgery), you must graduate from college and then go on to a four-year dental school program. The courses are similar to those medical students take and involve long hours of concentrated study. But the personal rewards are gratifying. To achieve takes time, patience, and the ability to accept frustration, but it builds moral fiber. If you can apply yourself and keep your objective firmly in front of you, you will find that dentistry is a most worthwhile career.

Further guidance can be obtained from the following:

American Association of Dental Schools
211 East Chicago Avenue
Chicago, Illinois 60611

American Dental Association
211 East Chicago Avenue
Chicago, Illinois 60611

THE PHYSICIAN'S ASSISTANT

There is a new career on the health horizon. It is a result of a major change in the way medical services are being made available to the entire country. We are in the era of the physician's assistant (P.A.).

Because of the need for adequate health care in the inner cities and the rural sections of the nation, this special kind of role had to be created. In particular, the P.A. promises to bridge the gap between city and country health facilities. Outlying areas do not have nearly enough doctors and nurses. Doctors who are practicing in small towns are overloaded. They can't possibly handle the demand for better service. However, the physician's assistant can take over much of the doctor's present chores.

President Nixon gave impetus to the P.A. program by asking for millions of dollars to finance it. A special government office has been established to handle the funds and their allocation. The Veterans Administration and the armed services are thinking about starting their own programs.

The P.A. bandwagon has caught on. The public is dissatisfied with the present situation, in which only the rich can face the disaster of a serious illness without facing financial disaster as well. Those living in nonurban

Climbing Up the Medical Ladder

areas are seriously affected by the lack of trained physicians and nurses. The physician's assistant fills this need.

It is obvious that most of the physician's routine office work can be done by a trained P.A., who takes the initial interview, examines the patient, and makes a preliminary diagnosis. The corpsmen in the armed services functioned beautifully during wartime and showed what men can do under stress after an intensive course in treating the wounded. Many of these ex-G.I.'s are now in P.A. programs.

For the physician P.A.'s are a great asset. He is free to devote his time to more complicated cases; he can increase his case load, and he has time to devote to research and additional education. When a doctor is under pressure to give a hasty examination, he can miss a vital diagnosis. With a physician's assistant helping him in his office, he knows that he will be able to offer a more comprehensive examination and additional services. His assistant has more time to listen and talk with the patient; thus, because of his all-around effectiveness, his inclusion on the health team will result in better medical care at a lower cost.

Obviously, not everyone can go to medical school, even with talent and academic ability. It is costly and involves long, hard years of study before the fledgling M.D. can begin to earn a living. The P.A. program is an ideal way to overcome these obstacles and to help the dedicated make a useful contribution to society.

Many nurses, who are currently practicing in hospitals and feel that their talents are not being utilized to their fullest, can now consider becoming physician's assistants. They have the basic skills, knowledge, and experience. They know how doctors work and are used to carrying out doctors' orders. For them it is an easy transition into the P.A. program.

There are several different specialty areas that the physician's assistant can choose from. First, you can become a physician's assistant, or associate, in pediatrics. Or you can decide upon general medicine, surgery, or obstetrics and gynecology. There are also programs in orthopedics and urology. Each specialty requires that the assistant successfully complete a two-year program in an approved P.A. course. Studies have shown that most medical training programs can be shortened without sacrificing quality.

You may also hear the term physician's associate. "Assistant" and "associate" are used interchangeably, but each state has its own requirements for registration. The first physician's-associate program began on the campus of Duke University in the 1960's. It is a two-year course after which the graduates work with family doctors, performing the following functions:

1. Taking a complete medical history.
2. Doing a thorough physical examination.
3. Giving injections.
4. Doing electrocardiograms.
5. Taking out sutures and foreign bodies.
6. Giving local anesthetics.
7. Reading Tine tests for TB and other skin tests.
8. Splinting sprains.
9. Incising skin abscesses.

These are just a few of the P.A.'s skills. Many of them are already performed by the nurse, and though there is controversy about the nurse's relationship to the P.A.

Climbing Up the Medical Ladder

program, it is easy to see how a nurse could assume these responsibilities.

The American Medical Association is currently evaluating P.A. programs with the objective of standardizing them and establishing criteria for licensing graduates. They have worked with medical specialty groups, such as the American Society of Internal Medicine and the American College of Surgeons, and have developed guidelines for each specialty.

There are approximately two hundred physician's assistants practicing at the present time. This new medical breed will bring health care of a high quality to a country sorely in need of expanding health services. You can be one of them, in a career with a real future.

Physician's Assistant Programs:

> Department of Medicine
> University of Alabama
> Birmingham, Alabama   35233

> Mercy Hospital and Medical Center
> 4077 Fifth Avenue
> San Diego, California   92103

> Stanford University Medical Center
> Stanford, California   94305

> University of Colorado
> 4200 East Ninth Avenue
> Denver, Colorado   80220

> Yale University
> School of Medicine
> 333 Cedar Street
> New Haven, Connecticut   06510

Grady Memorial Hospital
80 Butler Street, S.E.
Atlanta, Georgia   30303

Dartmouth Medical School
Hanover, New Hampshire   03755

Medex Program
P. O. Box 146
Nugget Arcade
Hanover, New Hampshire   03755

Brooklyn-Cumberland Medical Center
121 DeKalb Avenue
Brooklyn, New York   11201

State University of New York at Stony Brook
Health Sciences Center
Stony Brook, New York   11790

Hudson Valley Community College
80 Vandenburgh Avenue
Troy, New York   12180

Duke University Medical Center
P. O. Box 2914 CHS
Durham, North Carolina   27710

University of North Dakota
School of Medicine
1600 University Avenue
Grand Forks, North Dakota   58201

Cincinnati Technical College
3520 Central Parkway
Cincinnati, Ohio   45223

Clinical Corpsmen Program
The Cleveland Clinic Hospital
2020 East 93rd Street
Cleveland, Ohio   44106

University of Oklahoma
Medical Center
800 N. E. Fifteenth Street
Oklahoma City, Oklahoma 73104

Hahnemann Medical College of
 Allied Health Sciences
230 North Broad Street
Philadelphia, Pennsylvania 19102

University of Texas
Medical Branch
Galveston, Texas 77550

University of Washington
School of Medicine
444 N. E. Ravenna Boulevard
Seattle, Washington 98105

Alderson-Broaddus College
Philippi, West Virginia 26416

9.
The Most Noble Profession — The Doctor

> Medicine is, of all professions, the most noble; and yet through ignorance of those who practice it and of those who judge it superficially, it is now degraded to its lowest rank. So false a judgment seems to me to depend principally upon this—that in the cities, the profession of medicine is the only one that is subjected to no restriction, or punishment, except disgrace—now disgrace does not wound those who live by it. These people are very much like the characters who figure in tragedies; just as these characters have the appearance, the costumes, and the masques of actors, without being actors, so among physicians many are so by their titles, but very few are so, in fact.

So wrote Hippocrates, the father of modern medicine, in 300 B.C. It seems incredible that these words were written by an ancient Greek more than two thousand years ago. Yet Hippocrates lived during Greece's most brilliant age, and his thoughts are remarkably valid today when we consider the temptations of modern man in a society struggling to reclaim its lost values. To be a doctor is a profession that calls upon man's highest moral virtues. It requires intelligence, dedication, and spiritual and moral discipline.

The Most Noble Profession—The Doctor

Doctors, like all of us, are human beings, and they are subject to the same conflicts as other men. But generally they have a higher goal, a beautiful ideal, which impels many of them to resist selfish considerations and to serve humanity with skill and compassion. It is this quality that is ennobling. It is this dimension that sets them apart in moments of crisis so that most of us think of the physician as a true healer of men's bodies, minds, and spirits.

Since ancient Greece, the physician has always been held in great esteem. Homer wrote about a famous physician of the time called Machaon:

> A wise physician, skilled in our wounds to heal,
> Is more than armies to the public weal.

And the famous Aristotle said in praising Hippocrates:

> When we speak of the great Hippocrates, it is understood that we mean not the man, but the physician.

Homer, writing of the physicians of his day, said:

> Of two famed surgeons, Podaleirius stands
> This hour surrounded by the Trojan bands—
> And great Machaon, wounded in his tent,
> Now wants the succor so oft he lent.

The brilliant men of ancient Greece were philosophers and physicians. Like our most gifted professors, they developed a highly sophisticated culture dedicated to scholarship and learning. The physicians—priest physicians during Hippocrates' time—were called Asclepiads and practiced the healing art in the temples of Aesculapius. As in our own culture, medicine was considered the highest achievement. Perhaps that is why today we still feel a kind of awe when we think about the men who choose it as a career. The word "doctor" makes us stop and give pause. There is a feeling of respect and admiration surrounding that hard-won title.

The education of a physician is a long and difficult road. Many people take for granted the knowledge of their family physician. They forget the hours of study, frustration, and often deprivation that the young medical students must go through during their baptism in the medical world. There is also the ever-present sense of responsibility, which the student carries from the moment he or she enters medical school. Everything the student learns becomes a part of his being and from it he must draw when his real experience as a physician begins—the first day he walks into a hospital ward. The old man lying there, clinging to life, grasps the young doctor's hand with hope, trust, and faith. It is then that the tests, the trials, begin.

Perhaps to you a career as a doctor may seem like the most impossible of all the impossible dreams. And of course it is difficult, but it is not impossible. Are you ready to make the sacrifices necessary to fulfill that dream? Do you have stamina, dedication, ideals, and the self-discipline to withstand many obstacles without yielding to discouragement? If the answer is yes, then do it. Become a doctor.

How and where do you begin? In high school. Medicine must grab you, take over your life, fill you with a desire to devote yourself to its demands wholly and completely.

The Most Noble Profession—The Doctor

You must plan. And the way to do it is by taking those college prep courses that will prepare you for premed and then medical school. Science courses are essential. In addition to the essential knowledge they provide, they also sharpen your powers of observation, teach you objectivity. It is extremely important to develop these qualities, for they are indispensable to the physician.

Your four-year high school program should include three years of lab science, physics, biology, and chemistry. Math is extremely important, particularly algebra and geometry and calculus, if your school has advanced math courses. Most premed programs advise that you take history, political science, and sociology. Psychology is also helpful and, of course, four years of English. The foreign-language requirement varies with different colleges, but German, French, or Latin is recommended.

Many high schools now have "future doctors clubs." These groups are of great value, and if your school has one, you should plan on taking an active part in it. As a member of a future doctors club, you will have the opportunity to meet and talk with outstanding practitioners in your area. There will be lectures, discussions, and trips to hospitals, where you can get an idea of what the life of a physician is all about. It is an excellent way to bolster your ambitions and build self-confidence. Listening to experienced professionals talk about their work can teach you invaluable lessons and warn you about the pitfalls. And there is the warm feeling of sharing ideas in a setting of fellowship and intellectual stimulation.

A top-notch record in high school is absolutely mandatory for anyone who wants to go to medical school. The competition is great, and the demands of medical training require a well-disciplined, rational mind. Therefore, it is important that you make sure you develop your potential to the fullest extent, study hard, and approach application to college with a sober, objective viewpoint.

With such a goal in mind, it is best to seek advice on the right college for you from a guidance counselor who knows your capacities and the kind of person you are. Naturally, you and your parents have to assess the family's financial picture, too. The training of a doctor is an expensive undertaking, and it is wise to discuss these matters frankly so that you will be equipped to make the right choice. Also, it is a good idea to decide whether you want to go to a small college or a large university. Both can be first-rate academically. Are you the kind of person who prefers a small, closely knit school, where there is a warm, personal, family feeling? Or does a university with its varied intellectual and cultural activities turn you on? This is a major point to consider.

But no matter what type of college you choose, make sure it is accredited by the American Council on Education. Also, it is a good idea to check thoroughly into the premedical program and make sure the courses will give you the requirements needed for entrance into a good medical school. Science must be emphasized, and the best possible laboratory equipment and other teaching aids should be available. You can check the standards of the college by referring to a guide, *Universities and Colleges in the United States*. Your school should have a copy. It is a good reference to the accredited colleges in the country. Be certain the school you select has a good choice of subjects in the arts and humanities as well as science so that you will not get a lopsided education.

Although many students elect to take the three-year premed course, it is better by far to put in the additional year and get your bachelor's degree. Medical school standards are tough to meet. The extra time you will spend will be well worth it, if you want to stack up favorably against the competition.

Once you have made it to college, you should be sure to check with the premed adviser about the courses to take. It is extremely important to keep in close contact with those people on campus who advise students in the premed program. They can save you much heartache later on. Often students do not seek guidance from the right sources and discover too late that they have not enrolled in the requisite courses. So be smart. Check carefully.

Usually, premed programs feature physics, biology, chemistry, both organic and inorganic, and a great deal of lab practice. Math is also important, particularly higher mathematics, including calculus. Most medical schools require English and courses in the humanities.

By all means look into the various medical schools so that you will be prepared to make your application in your junior year. You should know the school's requirements and make certain that you are taking the prescribed courses.

If you do well in college and have the best possible preparation, chances are very good that you will be accepted in medical school. Obviously, the student who lags behind and allows off-campus temptations to lure him away from his studies will find it extremely difficult to be accepted. Only the student with good grades and the scholastic evidence to support his candidacy will be the one to make it. The choice of who gets in and who doesn't is always a thorny process of selection for any medical school admissions committee. Every applicant is given serious consideration. His scholastic standing, academic achievement, character, and participation in extracurricular activities are all weighed carefully.

Before applying to medical school, you should talk things over with your adviser and select those schools in which you have the best chance of gaining acceptance and those that offer a program most suitable for you. Consider finances and the school's location. If money is a problem, try to aim for a medical school in your hometown so that you can save on room and board.

Approved schools have met the criteria of the A.M.A. and the Association of American Medical Colleges. Once you have applied, you will have to take a special test. This test is the Medical College Admission Test.

So you have made your choice of several medical schools, sent in your application, and passed the medical admission test with a respectable score. Now you wait. You agonize and wonder if you have made it. Then one day the letter comes, the letter you have been waiting for, the letter that spells out the future you have so carefully planned. You have been accepted! Another hurdle has been vaulted. You are really on your way to becoming a physician.

And now the tough work begins. You will be immersed in many fascinating subjects, not only concerning the human body but the mind and soul as well. You will be studying man in his relationship to other men, the world he lives in, and space beyond. The four exciting years ahead include anatomy and physiology, biochemistry, pathology, lab analysis, microbiology, medicine, surgery, diagnosis, medical ethics, obstetrics and gynecology, and all of the other specialities.

During the last two years there is supervised clinical experience in the hospital with which the medical school is affiliated. There the student is assigned patients and begins to integrate what he has learned in the classroom with clinical practice.

The cost of four years of medical school varies, depending upon whether the school is a private institution or is state-run. A private medical school will cost approximately $14,000 to $15,000 for the four years, a state school a little over $8,000—more if you are a nonresident of the state. But you can now finance your education through a foundation of the A.M.A., which permits you to borrow the full amount and makes generous arrangements for you to pay back funds after you have become a doctor.

A doctor. Imagine what it must be like after those four years of medical school have been completed, and you approach graduation. Think of yourself at that final, majestic, rather noble ceremony, when you are awarded the M.D., Doctor of Medicine. It is appropriate to pause and contemplate the true meaning and value of that distinguished diploma and what it represents. For at that moment you may be called upon to take a solemn oath, to remind yourself of the spiritual and moral values inherent in the awarding of that degree, the Hippocratic Oath. It is still a beautiful and relevant document today, and expresses the highest ideals of the ancient Greek physician. All doctors should read it again in moments of doubt, cynicism, and weariness.

> I swear by Apollo the physician, by Aesculapius, by Hygiea and Panacea; by all the gods and goddesses—making them my witnesses, that I will with my strength and capacity, carry out this oath and engagement. I will plan my master in medicine in the same rank with the authors of my life; I will teach it to them without pay. I will communicate my precepts, my oral lessons, and all other instructions, to my sons, and to the sons of my master, and to those disciples who are bound by an engagement and an oath, according to the medical law, but to no others. I will direct the regimen of my patients, for their advantage to the best of my ability and my judgment. I will abstain from all wrong and all injustice. I will not furnish poison to anyone who solicits it, neither will I make suggestion of it to anyone; neither will I furnish to any woman an abortive. I will exercise my art, in innocency and purity. . . .
>
> Into whatever house I enter, it shall be for the good of my patient, keeping myself from all corrupting conduct and especially from the seduction of women and boys. . . . Whatever I see or hear in society, in the exercises and even not in the exercises of my profession, I will keep secret, if it is not necessary to divulge it, regarding discretion as a duty in all such cases.
>
> If I fulfill this oath, without violation, may it be given to me to enjoy happily life and my profession, honored forever among men; if I violate it, and perjure myself, let the opposite fate be my lot.

These words are sobering comments on a profession that demands the highest dedication from those who practice it. But men and women, human as they are, often succumb to less noble temptations. Still, standards and ideals are important to aspire to, and every young man or woman who wants to be a doctor should read the words of Hippocrates and realize that these values can help him reach the noblest achievements.

As a physician you can expect to have an income of over $35,000 a year. Even considering the financial investment of your education, it is a profession that rewards its practitioners generously.

More information concerning medical schools can be obtained from the following:

>American Medical Association
>535 North Dearborn Street
>Chicago, Illinois   60610

>National Medical Fellowships
>3935 Elm Street
>Downers Grove, Illinois   60515

>American Medical Women's
>   Association
>1740 Broadway
>New York, New York   10019

Medical Schools

The following list is a partial sampling of medical schools throughout the country. A complete listing can be obtained through the A.M.A.

>University of Alabama
>School of Medicine
>Birmingham, Alabama   35233
>public school

University of Arizona
College of Medicine
Tucson, Arizona   85724
public school

University of Arkansas
School of Medicine
Little Rock, Arkansas   72201
public school

University of California at Los Angeles
School of Medicine
Los Angeles, California   90024
public school

University of Southern California
School of Medicine
Los Angeles, California   90033
private school

University of California
School of Medicine S-211
San Francisco, California   94122
public school

Stanford University
School of Medicine
Stanford, California   94305
private school

University of Colorado
School of Medicine
Denver, Colorado   80220
public school

Yale University
School of Medicine
New Haven, Connecticut   06510
private school

Georgetown University
School of Medicine
Washington, D.C. 20007
private school

Howard University
College of Medicine
Washington, D.C. 20001
private school

University of Florida
College of Medicine
Gainesville, Florida 32601
public school

University of Miami
School of Medicine
Biscayne Annex
Miami, Florida 33152
private school

Emory University
School of Medicine
Atlanta, Georgia 30322
private school

Medical College of Georgia
Augusta, Georgia 30902
public school

Northwestern University
Medical School
Chicago, Illinois 60611
private school

University of Chicago
Pritzker School of Medicine
Chicago, Illinois 60637
private school

Indiana University
School of Medicine
Indianapolis, Indiana 46202
public school

University of Iowa
College of Medicine
Iowa City, Iowa 52240
public school

University of Kansas
School of Medicine
Kansas City, Kansas 66103
public school

University of Kentucky
College of Medicine
Lexington, Kentucky 40506
public school

Louisiana State University
School of Medicine
New Orleans, Louisiana 70112
private school

Tulane University
School of Medicine
New Orleans, Louisiana 70112
private school

Johns Hopkins University
School of Medicine
Baltimore, Maryland 21218
private school

Harvard Medical School
Boston, Massachusetts 02115
private school

Tufts University
School of Medicine
Boston, Massachusetts 02111
private school

University of Michigan
Medical School
Ann Arbor, Michigan 48104
public school

University of Minnesota
Medical School
Minneapolis, Minnesota 55455
public school

University of Missouri
Columbia School of Medicine
Columbia, Missouri 65201
public school

Saint Louis University
School of Medicine
St. Louis, Missouri 63104
private school

Washington University
School of Medicine
St. Louis, Missouri 63110
private school

University of Nebraska
College of Medicine
Omaha, Nebraska 68105
public school

New Jersey College of Medicine and Dentistry
New Jersey Medical School
Newark, New Jersey 07103
public school

University of New Mexico
School of Medicine
Albuquerque, New Mexico 87106
public school

Albany Medical College
Union University
Albany, New York 12208
private school

Albert Einstein College of Medicine
Yeshiva University
1300 Morris Park Avenue
Bronx, New York 10461
private school

State University of New York
Downstate Medical Center
College of Medicine
Brooklyn, New York 11226
public school

State University of New York at Buffalo
School of Medicine
Buffalo, New York 14214
public school

Cornell University
Medical College
Ithaca, New York 14850
private school

Columbia University
College of Physicians and Surgeons
New York, New York 10032
private school

Mount Sinai School of Medicine
1212 Fifth Avenue
New York, New York 10029
private school

New York University
School of Medicine
550 First Avenue
New York, New York 10016
private school

University of North Carolina
School of Medicine
Chapel Hill, North Carolina 27514
public school

Duke University
School of Medicine
Durham, North Carolina 27710
private school

University of Cincinnati
College of Medicine
Cincinnati, Ohio 45219
public school

University of Oregon
Medical School
Portland, Oregon 97201
public school

Hahnemann Medical College of Philadelphia
Philadelphia, Pennsylvania 19102
private school

Thomas Jefferson University
Jefferson Medical College
Philadelphia, Pennsylvania 19107
private school

Temple University
School of Medicine
Philadelphia, Pennsylvania 19140
private school

University of Pennsylvania
School of Medicine
Philadelphia, Pennsylvania   19104
private school

University of Tennessee
College of Medicine
Memphis, Tennessee   38103
public school

Meharry Medical College
School of Medicine
Nashville, Tennessee   37208
private school

University of Texas
Medical Branch
Galveston, Texas   77550
public school

Baylor College of Medicine
Houston, Texas   77025
private school

University of Vermont
College of Medicine
Burlington, Vermont   05401
public school

University of Washington
School of Medicine
Seattle, Washington   98105
public school

University of Wisconsin
Medical School
Madison, Wisconsin   53706
public school

10.
The Practice of the Healing Art

The day you graduate from medical school, your apprenticeship has just begun. As an intern you will begin the real practice of medicine—in the wards of a hospital. For this experience you will be paid an average of $6,000 a year. Residents, those doctors who are training for specialization in a particular branch of medicine, are paid up to $12,000 a year, depending upon where they are working.

THE INTERN

Most medical school graduates wisely choose a rotating internship. This covers a year's time, in which the intern has the opportunity to gain valuable experience in surgery, medicine, pediatrics, obstetrics and gynecology, the emergency room, and other services. Experience of this nature gives the young intern a broad field of knowledge. He learns to use his basic tools and puts into practice all he has studied. He gets to know the hospital routine; he develops confidence and an ability to handle patients.

The year he serves as an intern is a most enlightening experience for the young doctor. This is real medicine; he is no longer in a classroom. Life and death are involved now—the eternal struggle, with all the unanswerable questions a doctor must agonize over alone in his own skull. He will know much frustration, but he will also have the satisfaction of meeting the tests and challenges of a profession he has fought hard to enter.

THE RESIDENT

After the internship, the young doctor usually decides to continue training in one of the many specialties open to him. This period of training is called the residency. It takes from two to five years, depending upon the hospital and the specialty.

Just what does the resident doctor do? What are his responsibilities? For one thing, the interns are always under the supervision of the chief resident. All resident doctors have a great deal of contact with patients.

The resident must attend and take part in many hospital staff conferences, where the attending physicians do much of the teaching. He must exercise independent judgment concerning the diagnoses of his patients' illnesses. Naturally, the resident must be responsible to the attending physician who supervises him, particularly when there is a difficult case and a disagreement over the best way to handle it. The surgical resident does major surgical procedures and even performs many different types of operations. This is an extremely important part of his growth as a surgeon.

The hospital's instructors, practicing physicians who have passed examinations in their specialty areas, teach residents at the bedside. This gives the resident on-the-spot clinical experience. He also takes part in "grand rounds," conferences with lectures and seminars and where interesting cases are presented—often by him.

The Practice of the Healing Art

Most hospitals have scheduled clinicopathology conferences where the residents take an active part in preparing the program. Many specialists are involved in these presentations. It gives the resident the opportunity to see the correlation between the patient's disease and the pathologic findings. He can learn a great deal from these cases.

Another important feature of resident training is the time the resident spends in the hospital's clinics, or outpatient department. Here he can test his skill at making a correct diagnosis. In a big-city hospital such experience is invaluable. In the clinic he will come into contact with patients from a variety of cultural backgrounds. He must be able to relate to people and understand them and learn to use his qualities of compassion and human concern.

Often the resident follows up his own patients. He may make the initial diagnosis, admit the patient to the hospital, and then perform the necessary surgery. This kind of experience also prepares the resident for private practice later on, as it gives him the basic skills he will need.

Emergency-room experience is also an important dimension to the resident's training. Here he learns to handle all types of emergencies—trauma, heart attacks, G.I. (gastrointestinal) bleeders, sickle cell crises, and many others. He perfects his ability to make the right diagnosis under trying circumstances and learns to make decisions. This type of experience also strengthens his self-confidence.

In the operating room, the fledgling surgeon must have responsibility so he can develop his technique. Sufficient experience in assuming responsibility for major surgical cases is essential if he is to refine the skill and judgment he will need as a surgeon.

Residency requirements are set up by an accrediting board, the Council of Medical Education of the A.M.A. Each specialty has its own rules for training. For example, let's take the resident in surgery. His period of training must be approved not only by the A.M.A. but by the American College of Surgeons and the American Board of Surgery. Four years of surgical experience is considered necessary by these groups.

To be certified and become a Fellow in the American College of Surgeons, the surgical resident, after completing training, must take the examination and pass it.

SPECIALIZATION

Within surgery there are, of course, many specialties from which to choose. This holds true for other areas, such as medicine. Many M.D.'s who are called internists specialize further as cardiologists or experts in some other field.

What kind of specialist do you think you want to be? Pathologist? Anesthesiologist? Pediatrician? General practitioner? Psychiatrist? Surgeon? Internist? Dermatologist? Ophthalmologist?

Here are some of the areas of specialization you might select:

Internal Medicine

The internist is proficient at diagnosing and treating medical disorders of the various organs of the body.

The Practice of the Healing Art

General Practitioner (G.P.)

Better known as the family doctor, the G.P. deals with the general illnesses and problems of the patient, providing medical care, diagnosis, and treatment in many areas of medicine, and making referrals to specialists when necessary.

Obstetrics and Gynecology

This specialty deals with the female body and the treatment of the diseases that affect it. Obstetricians provide care during pregnancy and delivery.

Pediatrics

The pediatrician is concerned with the diagnosis and treatment of diseases of children.

Anesthesiology

The anesthesiologist gives anesthetic agents to patients during surgery.

Neurology

Neurology involves the diagnosis and treatment of disorders of the brain and the nervous system.

Dermatology

This specialty has to do with skin diseases, their diagnosis and treatment.

Ophthalmology

The ophthalmologist diagnoses eye diseases and also performs eye surgery.

Orthopedics

Orthopedics relates to the bones, the diagnosis and treatment of bone diseases, fractures, and their treatment by surgical methods.

Pathology

This field is concerned with the cells and tissues of the body and their study as it relates to disease.

Plastic Surgery

This surgical specialty is involved with reconstructing deformed areas of the body and also performing surgery for cosmetic purposes.

Psychiatry

This branch of medicine is concerned with the understanding of mental disorders and their treatment.

Radiology

This specialty deals with the interpretation of X rays in relation to disease and is also involved with radioactive substances, radium, cobalt, and isotopes.

Urology

The urologist diagnoses and treats those diseases that affect the genitourinary system.

There are many other specialties, but these are the main areas. Each has its own requirements for Board Certification, and the residency training periods vary somewhat from hospital to hospital.

THE CARDIAC SURGEON

Many new areas for specialization have developed in the past several years. Cardiac surgery, for example, is a highly skilled technique practiced by the most competent surgeons. Hospitals usually have on their staffs one or two of these unique men who perform open-heart surgery. They do this specialized work after serving a general surgical residency at those institutions that offer experience in cardiovascular surgery. These doctors must have satisfactory experience in thoracic surgery as well.

To practice cardiovascular surgery, the physician must be certified by the American Board of Thoracic Surgery. Here, the team concept comes into play. The Board has determined certain guidelines for the cardiac surgeon, and teamwork is one of the most important. Therefore, hospitals that are equipped to perform this intricate type of surgery have a cardiovascular team.

For example a special O.R. setup is needed. The nurses specifically trained as cardiovascular scrub nurses should have sufficient experience to maintain the highest standards of technique. The special equipment and instruments must always be in perfect working order and are subject to scrupulous inspection by the Head Nurse. The heart-lung machine is a major fixture in the cardiovascular unit, and only the most competent operator is allowed to handle it during surgery. The cardiac surgeon also must have top-notch liaison facilities at his disposal in the hospital. Nurses in the intensive care unit need additional training to be able to care for patients postoperatively. Everyone must work together as a team to ensure the best possible chance for the patient's recovery. In addition, the surgeon needs laboratory, radiological, and other assistance to help him carry out his complex job.

Cardiac surgery is one of the relatively new areas of specialization and it is certainly one of the most exciting and tense. The cardiac surgeon must have great technical skill, a cool head, and the ability to cope with tremendous pressure. The responsibility he faces every moment he is in the operating room is a great burden. Try to imagine what it might be like to realize with every operation that life or death lies in your hands. Certainly these men and women, as well as doctors in the rest of medicine's specialties, deserve our respect for their skill, talent, and courage.

THE TRANSPLANT SURGEON

The same situation holds true for the transplant surgeon. Today kidney transplants, for example, are becoming more and more refined, but the transplant surgeon still faces great risks in his work because of the possibility of tissue rejection or infection in the transplant recipient. Here, too, special teams are required so that the surgery can be performed under the most advantageous circumstances.

In order to record transplant surgery and make documented case material available to transplant surgeons, these three groups have been initiated:

1. EDTA—The European Dialysis and Transplant Association
2. Human Renal Transplant Registry
3. National Australian Renal Transplantation Subcommittee

From these groups and the master data bank, Vogelbank Computing Center of Northwestern University, surgeons can quickly get valuable statistics and information concerning transplant surgery to guide them with their own problems.

Transplant surgery is also being tried in lung, bone marrow, and even liver disease. The future promises to refine these revolutionary procedures and to solve the problems of rejection and infection.

SPACE MEDICINE

Another exciting area in medicine is space medicine. At Houston, Texas, physicians are studying the astronauts and their physiological reactions to space travel. What effects does the lunar atmosphere, as an example, have on a man's cardiovascular system? On his nervous and digestive system? Can man survive life in space for an extended period of time? Is there a radiation threat?

How does his body react to the different atmospheric conditions?

These and many other scientific questions are being explored through space medicine, a new specialty in medicine. It offers a challenge to space-minded, adventurous young doctors who want to try the new and unexplored territory in their profession.

The field of medicine will always need dedicated young men and women who want to make a real contribution to humanity. As Hippocrates said, it is the noblest of professions, and that is so because of the physicians who are ennobled by it.

Additional Reference Sources

>American Society of Internal Medicine
>525 The Hearst Building
>3rd at Market Street
>San Francisco, California   94103

>American Association of Ophthalmology
>1100 Seventeenth Street, N.W.
>Washington, D.C.   20036

>American Psychiatric Association
>1700 Eighteenth Street, N.W.
>Washington, D.C.   20009

>American Public Health Association
>1015 Seventeenth Street, N.W.
>Washington, D.C.   20036

>Association of American Medical Colleges
>1 Dupont Circle, N.W.
>Washington, D.C.   20036

National Honor Society
National Association of Secondary
School Principals
1201 Sixteenth Street, N.W.
Washington, D.C. 20036

National Medical Association
2109 "E" Street, N.W.
Washington, D.C. 20036

Science Talent Search
1719 North Street, N.W.
Washington, D.C. 20036

American Board of Orthopedic Surgery
430 North Michigan Avenue
Chicago, Illinois 60611

American College of Obstetricians
 and Gynecologists
79 West Monroe Street
Chicago, Illinois 60603

American College of Radiology
20 North Wacker Drive
Chicago, Illinois 60606

American College of Surgeons
55 East Erie Street
Chicago, Illinois 60611

American Society of Clinical Pathologists
2100 West Harrison Street
Chicago, Illinois 60612

National Medical Fellowships for
Black Students
3935 Elm Street
Downers Grove, Illinois 60515

American Academy of Pediatrics
1801 Hinman Avenue
Evanston, Illinois 60204

National Merit Scholarship Corporation
990 Grove Street
Evanston, Illinois 60201

Society of Nuclear Medical Technologists
1201 Waukegan Road
Glenview, Illinois 60025

American Society of Anesthesiologists
515 Busse Highway
Park Ridge, Illinois 60068

American Society for Pharmacology and
  Experimental Therapeutics
9650 Rockville Pike
Bethesda, Maryland 20014

American Academy of Family Physicians
Volker Boulevard at Brookside
Kansas City, Missouri 64112

American Diabetes Association
18 East 48th Street
New York, New York 10017

American Heart Association
44 East 23rd Street
New York, New York 10010

11.
Your Place on the Team

As you can see, the possibilities for a career in medicine are unlimited. So why not use your energy and talent and your desire to help others, and join the health team? Make a real contribution to your community in a respected, well-paying profession.

First, take an objective look at your assets. What are your interests? Your strengths and weaknesses? Where do you want to work—city or country? Big hospital—small hospital? Public agency or neighborhood health center? Write it down. Then match your responses with the health career that most closely fits your abilities and requirements.

For example, if you possess manual dexterity and a fanatic's love of detail, then the career for you is medical technology. On the other hand, let's say math and chemistry are your weaknesses, but you have a strong urge to do something for others. In that case, consider becoming a mental health assistant. If, however, you combine a compassion for people with a natural flair for the sciences, nursing could be the perfect choice.

There is a great variety of careers. Once you've narrowed your selection to the careers that you are suited for, you can pick the one that appeals the most to you.

A major point to consider is whether you can reasonably expect to complete a four-year college course.

Even if that is not possible, chances are you will still find plenty of careers that will stimulate you. Remember, you can always return to school later on and complete your education. In the meantime, you will have a good, solid career and, most important, will gain experience to sharpen your skills and talents.

Bear in mind that if nursing is your main objective, you can attain it in a two-year A.A.S.-degree program, or in one year if you become a licensed practical nurse. That is where good nursing really counts—at the bedside, not behind a desk. You will have the opportunity to give to others in a meaningful, human situation, where your skill can mean the difference between prolonged hospital care and recovery.

Lab careers offer a wide variety of exciting jobs. So do the areas of occupational health technician and recreational health technician, two fields that need young people with zest, drive, and artistic ability. When you get involved in your work, enjoy what you are doing, and are successful at it, the chance to perfect your skills is always available. Once you are established on the team, you can get your bachelor's degree and become an occupational therapist or a recreational therapist.

There are still other choices. Remember, you can be an inhalation therapist and save a life in the emergency room with your skilled C.P.R. technique. This is a career with a terrific future. Another exciting field, M.E.T. medical emergency technologist, may be just the right specialty, if you crave action and drama. You can also choose dietetics, dental hygiene, or medical records. All of these two-year programs can give you a career with a future.

For the college-bound and those determined to go beyond the bachelor's degree, there are excellent opportunities in optometry, dentistry, speech therapy, social work, and medicine.

THE PODIATRIST

In addition, there are several other health careers still to choose from. Have you ever considered podiatry? This is a growing field with top-level opportunities for anyone who genuinely cares about people and likes the sciences.

All of us have some type of foot problem during our lifetime. Perhaps it's a birth defect or a minor deformity. The podiatrist can help. If you become one, you can earn up to $20,000 a year.

As a practicing podiatrist, you are involved with foot care, the diagnosis and treatment of foot ailments, and health teaching. To earn the degree D.P.M., Doctor of Podiatric Medicine, you must first finish a two-year college program that is peppered generously with courses in the sciences—biology, chemistry, anatomy and physiology, bacteriology, and pathology. The rest of the course is another four years emphasizing clinical experience. Each state has different requirements, so it is important to check your state's licensing laws. The following schools offer podiatry courses:

>California College of Podiatric Medicine
>1770 Eddy Street
>San Francisco, California   94115

>Illinois College of Podiatric Medicine
>1327 North Clark Street
>Chicago, Illinois   60610

M. J. Lewi College of Podiatry
53–55 East 124th Street
New York, New York 10035

Ohio College of Podiatric Medicine
1057 Cornell Road
Cleveland, Ohio 44106

Pennsylvania College of Podiatric Medicine
Pine at Eighth Street
Philadelphia, Pennsylvania 19107

Also check with:

American Podiatry Association
20 Chevy Chase Circle, N.W.
Washington, D.C. 20015

THE PUBLIC HEALTH STATISTICIAN

Do you recall seeing movies where the department of epidemiology tracked down a rare disease and saved an unsuspecting victim's life? Public health offers many fascinating careers to those with the talents of a medical detective. Combining research and perseverance, the career of public health statistician can give you a most unusual future. Naturally, your strong point in high school must be math, because the public health statistician's tool is a computer-type brain.

What do these health statisticians do? They sort out important facts relating to the nation's health so that we can be aware of the effectiveness of the country's medical care. It is an interesting mix of taking facts, determining valuable statistics, and communicating all of these elements in a logical way.

As a health statistician you will be analyzing all kinds of health facts. For example, how many people in the 40–65 age group were cancer victims last year? Do more men than women die of cancer of the lung? What was the breakdown of live births in 1972 for women in the 18–30 childbearing years? What type of person is most prone to heart attacks or hypertension? Is there a personality picture of such a victim?

These and many other fascinating questions are grist for the public health statistician's detecting mill. In the pursuit of accurate answers you may be the person to formulate your own survey and send out detailed questionnaires to people all over the country. It is your job to find and synthesize health facts for the benefit of your community. Through your efforts as statistician, you can help improve the quality and delivery of medical care in this country.

As a fledgling in this field, you will probably earn approximately $8,000 a year—and considerably more if you develop your skills to a higher degree and gain additional education. The top-notch people earn over $25,000 a year.

Obviously, a career with this kind of skill requires graduation from a four-year baccalaureate program, bolstered with such subjects as statistics and math. For more information, contact:

>Society for Public Health Educators
>655 Sutter Street
>San Francisco, California   94102

>American Statistical Association
>806 Fifteenth Street, N.W.
>Washington, D.C.   20006

THE HEALTH TEACHER

If you have a strong desire to teach and you have a college degree, why not join the medical team as a health teacher?

It is the aim of the health teacher to inform, educate, and counsel the public in a nondirective way. The health teacher, for example, may be invited to set up a special program in a school and to guide leaders among parents and teachers who will put the plan into action. As a health educator, you will take an active role in making the community aware of those medical problems that can be solved through group action.

This is an important and challenging career. It takes a broad spectrum of talents to be successful as a health teacher. Bear in mind that to reach a top-level position, you will have to do graduate work and obtain a master's degree. The job also requires an ability to communicate. In other words, you will need a strong scientific background, a creative flair, and an ability to relate well to others so that you can develop rapport easily. Persuasiveness is an asset here, too.

As a health teacher you can influence many people. You will be asked to talk to groups about their ideas concerning health. If you are knowledgeable and sincere and know how to present all of the aspects of a health issue, you will be accomplishing a worthwhile purpose. For example, you might talk about sex education, venereal disease, drug addiction, or birth control. It's up to the health teacher to be honest, well informed, and positive in approach. Remember, as a health educator you represent an authority figure in the medical world. The group you are working with looks to you as the health-team leader. They want to hear your views on the problems that affect them and their children.

You will be called upon to help the community sort out the basic issues, whether they have to do with safety, mental health, prenatal care, or dental problems. Once you have presented a truthful picture of the situation, it is also up to you to offer a concrete and positive solution, which the community will then put into action.

Visiting with various groups in the community and getting to know the health problems they are most concerned with will make you a part of community affairs. By using a positive and helpful approach, you will provide the right answers to difficult problems.

The best way to prepare for a career in this exciting field is by taking an approved course in college for teachers, with a major in health. You will need a thorough grounding in science and in the social sciences—sociology, psychology, and anthropology—plus the regular liberal arts requirements. More information can be obtained from the following:

> Society for Public Health Education
> 655 Sutter Street
> San Francisco, California 94102

> American Public Health Association
> 1015 Eighteenth Street, N.W.
> Washington, D.C. 20036

> American Social Health Association
> 1740 Broadway
> New York, New York 10019

Columbia University
Teachers College
New York, New York 10027

Society of Public Health Educators
419 Park Avenue South
New York, New York 10016

THE PHARMACIST

When you go into a drugstore, do you ever stop to think about what it takes to become a pharmacist? Pharmacy is another important career. Many people spend a great deal of time in the local drugstore, shopping, talking to the pharmacist about their health problems and about the things on their mind generally.

Usually, the pharmacist is a very sympathetic person. His job also carries with it a high degree of responsibility. The pharmacist often is tempted by people who want drugs without a prescription and he must maintain his principles at all times. It is a demanding profession. He works long hours, and he must constantly be involved with the public. Some pharmacists practice their art in hospitals, and here, too, great demands are put upon them.

But the job has its rewards. The pharmacist's role is always changing, because he has to keep up with the enormous proliferation of new drugs. Not only that, he is also a teacher. People ask him for information. He must have a thorough knowledge of the drugs he is dispensing.

As a pharmacist you can earn more than $14,000 a year if you have the education and experience. If this field appeals to you, consider the educational requirements. A big plus in high school is a strong curriculum that stresses math and science. You must then complete the five-year college program in pharmacy in order to receive your license. In college, training as a pharmacist emphasizes chemistry, pharmacology, and math. Other courses are derived from the social sciences and humanities, but the major part of the program is concerned with drugs and their effects. If you are interested, the following sources can provide you with additional information:

> American Pharmaceutical Association
> 2215 Constitution Avenue, N.W.
> Washington, D.C. 20037

> American Society of Hospital Pharmacists
> 4630 Montgomery Avenue
> Washington, D.C. 20014

> American Association of
>   Colleges of Pharmacy
> 8121 Georgia Avenue
> Silver Spring, Maryland 20910

> American Society for Pharmacology
>   and Experimental Therapeutics
> 9650 Rockville Pike
> Bethesda, Maryland 20014

THE ENVIRONMENTAL TECHNICIAN

Perhaps you're an outdoorsy type of person. Is ecology your big interest? Then you can explore your ecological bent with a health career. Be an environmental technician. These people, who are vitally concerned with protecting our health from pollutants, acquire specimens of air, food, or water to be examined in the laboratory. They work with engineers and other public health technicians to preserve our environment.

Environmental technicians are needed in many different areas. There are jobs available in industry or public health agencies, and if you prefer a more rustic setting, there's a place for you in the agricultural field.

You can become an environmental technician via the two-year A.A.S.-degree route, with courses emphasizing the sciences, and earn up to $10,000 a year. And you can always get your bachelor's degree later on.

As an environmental technician you can satisfy your love for the outdoors as an "outdoor man" collecting specimens, or you can stick to the lab as an "inside man," studying and analyzing the air and water samples. Whichever you choose, you will help to preserve the health of a pollution-conscious community.

To find out more about this new career opportunity, write:

> National Environmental Health Association
> 1600 Pennsylvania Avenue
> Denver, Colorado 80203
>
> International Association of Milk,
> Food and Environmental Sanitarians
> P.O. Box 437, Blue Ridge Road
> Shelbyville, Indiana 46176

THE SANITARIAN

Working along with the environmental technicians are the sanitarians. These professionals are also concerned with public health standards. They work with public health agencies as inspectors, and to make sure that the public is not contaminated by faulty sewage or polluted water supplies, they investigate nursing homes, restaurants, plants, and sewage disposal units. If an infringement of the health standards is discovered, then it is up to the sanitarian to make sure the situation is corrected. The sanitarian also works with the sanitary engineers, the men who inspect sewage units and the public recreation buildings that house swimming pools. They inspect these areas in similar fashion to the sanitarian and make sure the health laws are enforced.

These careers average $10,000 a year, although those with more education and experience can command much higher salaries.

Sanitarians must have a baccalaureate degree; sanitary engineers need a baccalaureate degree in the engineering field. For more information, contact:

> National Environmental Health Association
> 1600 Pennsylvania Avenue
> Denver, Colorado 80203

> International Association of Milk,
> Food and Environmental Sanitarians
> P.O. Box 437, Blue Ridge Road
> Shelbyville, Indiana 46176

> American Academy of Environmental Engineers
> Box 1278
> Rockville, Maryland 20850

THE BIOMEDICAL EQUIPMENT TECHNICIAN

In the health field the career of biomedical equipment technician is new and unique. Haven't you wondered who takes care of all the complex hospital equipment, which must be ready for use at a moment's notice? Before that heart-lung machine goes into action, it is the biomedical equipment technician's responsibility to make sure it is in perfect working order. He or she is the person who knows how to operate this complicated machine. Also, he must be able to work with special cardiac monitors, the dialysis equipment used in kidney disease, and other finely sensitive instruments. This equipment can mean life or death to the patient, so the biomedical technician is vital to the health team.

These professionals may work with computers as well and should have training in programming. They also work in research units where new types of equipment are tested for hospital use. It is an interesting field for those with highly developed technical and mathematical skills, and has a bright future in the health career program.

To qualify as a biomedical equipment technician, you need a two-year A.A.S.-degree course, plus clinical training. You can work in industry or in a hospital. There are many excellent programs offered in this field, and for further solid information, contact:

> Alliance for Engineering in Medicine
>   and Biology
> 3900 Wisconsin Avenue, N.W.
> Suite N300
> Washington, D.C. 20016
>
> Biomedical Engineering Society
> P.O. Box 1600
> Evanston, Illinois 60204

Biomedical Engineering and
  Instrumentation Branch
DRS
National Institutes of Health
9000 Wisconsin Avenue
Bethesda, Maryland 20014

THE HOSPITAL ADMINISTRATOR

Perhaps your real capacities lie in your organizational talents. Have you ever considered the possibility of becoming a hospital administrator? Running a hospital is a varied and difficult job. If you fancy yourself as a high-powered administrator of a "white city," then think about the excitement of stepping into a top job as a health manager.

Right now there are seven thousand hospitals in the United States. Who is going to direct their activities? People like you—if this is your ambition. Competent managers are needed to keep pace with our growing health care system. Working with the hospital's board of directors, the administrator acts upon their plans for the smooth functioning of the hospital. Obviously, you need to know and develop talents in many different areas in order to be successful as a hospital administrator. Administrators must be organization people. They have to be able to set up workable plans so the hospital and all its various departments will run smoothly.

Think of the many different areas in a hospital! How can they operate—and cooperate? There are the various medical and surgical units, laboratories, kitchens, operating rooms, clinics—but the clever and well-organized hospital administrator can and does put them all together to spell efficiency.

The hospital administrator also represents the health team to the community, so he or she must be a kind of medical public relations man as well. His main concern, however, is the hospital. Is it running as it should? How does it compare in service and efficiency with other hospitals in the area? If it is slipping, what can and must be done to improve the coordination of its services to the public?

Most administrators can earn up to $18,000 a year. It is a good-paying job in a fast-growing and important industry—health.

For a career as a hospital administrator, a baccalaureate degree is essential, plus a master's degree, as well. The master's degree must be earned at a school with an accredited course in hospital administration. Clinical experience in a hospital is also required.

To find out more about a career in this field, contact the following:

> Association of University Programs
>   in Hospital Administration
> Room 420
> 1 Dupont Circle
> Washington, D.C.   20036
>
> American College of Hospital Administrators
> 840 North Lake Shore Drive
> Chicago, Illinois   60611
>
> American Hospital Association
> 840 North Lake Shore Drive
> Chicago, Illinois   60611

Cornell University
Sloan Institute of Hospital Administration
314 Malott Hall
Ithaca, New York   14850

This then is a roundup of health careers that offer exciting possibilities for the future—your future. The health team needs young people who have ideals, talent, and ambition—young people who want to put their energies into shape and form and direction. What better direction than helping others?

Regardless of how much one earns in a lifetime, the best rewards are those we derive from giving to others. As a skilled member of the health team you can have the warm, good feeling of helping the crippled to walk again, showing the mentally ill patient how to live again, or teaching a child to trust again. By joining the team you can learn the best way to serve your community. You will be helping those who need it—and yourself.

Appendix

YOUR PERSONAL HEALTH CAREER MATCH-MATE TESTS

TEST I *Check One*

                                                                           Yes No

1. Do you want to work in the city? ____ ____
2. Do you want to work in a big-city hospital? ____ ____
3. Do you have a passion for details? ____ ____
4. Are you good at math? ____ ____
5. Is science your strong point? ____ ____
6. Do you like to work independently? ____ ____
7. Are you well disciplined? ____ ____

TEST II

                                                                           Yes No

1. Would you prefer working in a rural area? ____ ____

Appendix

2. Do you like working with others? ___ ___
3. Are you an outgoing person? ___ ___
4. Is science your best subject? ___ ___
5. Can you express yourself well? ___ ___
6. Do you consider yourself to be understanding and compassionate? ___ ___
7. Are you a leader? ___ ___

TEST III

              Yes No

1. Do you rank in the top third of your class? ___ ___
2. Is science your major interest? ___ ___
3. Do you think you are a person with high ideals and dedication? ___ ___
4. Do obstacles fail to discourage you? ___ ___
5. Are you determined to get the best possible education and make sacrifices for it? ___ ___
6. Are you truly concerned with the welfare of others? ___ ___
7. Do you have good study habits? ___ ___

TEST IV

	Yes	No
1. Are you a creative person?	——	——
2. Do you enjoy being around people rather than working alone?	——	——
3. Is acting, painting, or music one of your favorite hobbies?	——	——
4. Are you able to exert your influence on others?	——	——
5. Do you like children?	——	——
6. Do you have a talent for teaching?	——	——
7. Do you think of yourself as a humanitarian?	——	——

TEST V

	Yes	No
1. Are you unsure about what you want to do after high school?	——	——
2. Are you anxious to start working as soon as possible—but wish to have a career?	——	——

3. Are you interested in social and health issues in your community? ⎯⎯ ⎯⎯
4. Do you have a *B* average, or higher, in your science courses? ⎯⎯ ⎯⎯
5. Can you study hard without getting angry or frustrated? ⎯⎯ ⎯⎯
6. Do you make friends easily? ⎯⎯ ⎯⎯
7. Do you feel good inside after doing something for someone else? ⎯⎯ ⎯⎯

If, in Test I, you answered yes to five out of the seven questions, then you would, in all probability, make a successful medical technologist. A career as a lab technician, cytotechnologist, or medical technologist would bring out your strong points and give you a great deal of personal satisfaction. On the other hand, if you responded negatively, chances are you are more of a "people-oriented" person. You probably scored higher on Test II or IV. Therefore, your career choices would include nursing, mental health assistant, occupational therapist, recreation therapist, or speech therapist.

If you answered yes to five or more of the questions in Test II, you would make an excellent nursing candidate, particularly in community nursing. You would also fit into most of the two-year health careers emphasizing patient contact.

A majority of yeses in Test III indicates that medicine

is a strong choice for you. Negative responses show that you would be more suited to one of the two-year programs.

Positive answers to five or more questions in Test IV highlight the creative, imaginative person who would do well in the occupational and recreational fields.

Five or more yes responses in Test V mean that you are a good bet for any of the two-year health programs, if you have a strong sense of purpose and motivation.

Test your career choices by using the guide at the end of this section, too.

HANDY HEALTH CAREER GUIDE

Beyond the Baccalaureate

> Dentistry
> Hospital administration
> Medicine
> Optometry
> Pharmacy
> Psychiatric social work
> Speech pathology

Baccalaureate Preparation

> Health educator
> Medical technologist
> Nursing
> Nutritionist
> Occupational therapist
> Physical therapist

Appendix

  Physician's associate
  Podiatrist
  Public health statistician
  Recreational therapist
  Sanitarian

A.A.S.-Degree Programs

  Biomedical equipment technician
  Certified laboratory assistant
  Cytotechnologist
  Dental hygienist
  Dental laboratory technician
  Dietetic technician assistant
  Environmental technician
  Histology technician
  Inhalation therapist
  Medical emergency technician
  Medical records technician
  Mental health assistant
  Nursing
  Operating room technician
  Occupational therapist assistant
  Physical therapist assistant
  Recreational therapist assistant
  X-ray technician

Special Certificate Program

  Physician's assistant
  Physician's associate

And Some More Health-Related Careers

Art therapist
Audiologist
Biochemist
Biophysicist
Biostatistician
Central service technician
Chemist
Electrocardiograph technician
Electroencephalograph technician
Health science librarian
Hospital engineer
Housekeeper
Laundry manager
Medical illustrator
Medical photographer
Microbiologist
Music therapist
Nurse anesthetist
Nurse midwife
Pathologist

COMPLETE GUIDE TO HEALTH ORGANIZATIONS

American Association for Inhalation Therapy
3554 Ninth Street
Riverside, California 92501

American Association for Health, Physical Education and Recreation
1201 Sixteenth Street, N.W.
Washington, D.C. 20036

Appendix

American Pharmaceutical Association
2215 Constitution Avenue, N.W.
Washington, D.C. 20037

American Rehabilitation Counseling Association
1607 New Hampshire Avenue, N.W.
Washington, D.C. 20009

American Society for Microbiology
1913 I Street, N.W.
Washington, D.C. 20006

Association of American Medical Colleges
1 Dupont Circle, N.W.
Washington, D.C. 20036

Association of Schools of Allied Health Professions
1 Dupont Circle
Suite 300
Washington, D.C. 20036

National Medical Association
1717 Massachusetts Avenue, N.W.
Washington, D.C. 20036

U.S. Office of Education
Division of Vocational and Technical Education
Health Occupations
400 Maryland Avenue, S.W.
Washington, D.C. 20202

Association of Medical Illustrators
c/o Medical Illustration Dept.
Medical College of Georgia
Augusta, Georgia 30902

American Academy of Physical Medicine and
  Rehabilitation
30 North Michigan Avenue
Chicago, Illinois 60602

American Association of Dental Schools
211 East Chicago Avenue
Chicago, Illinois 60611

American Association of Nurse Anesthetists
111 East Wacker Drive
Suite 929
Chicago, Illinois 60601

American Dental Assistants Association
211 East Chicago Avenue
Chicago, Illinois 60611

American Hospital Association
840 North Lake Shore Drive
Chicago, Illinois 60611

American Medical Association
535 North Dearborn Street
Chicago, Illinois 60610

American Medical Record Association
Suite 1850
875 North Michigan Avenue
Chicago, Illinois 60611

American Veterinary Medical Association
600 South Michigan Avenue
Chicago, Illinois 60605

Biomedical Engineering Society
P. O. Box 1600
Evanston, Illinois 60204

Appendix

American Society of Radiologic Technologists
645 North Michigan Avenue
Suite 620
Chicago, Illinois 60611

Medical Library Association
919 North Michigan Avenue
Suite 2023
Chicago, Illinois 60611

American Medical Technologists
710 Higgins Road
Park Ridge, Illinois 60068

American Society for Electroencephalographic Technologists
University of Iowa
Division of EEG and Neurophysiology
500 Newton Road
Iowa City, Iowa 52240

American Speech and Hearing Association
9030 Old Georgetown Road
Bethesda, Maryland 20014

MEDIHC Program
9000 Rockville Pike
Bethesda, Maryland 20014

National Committee for Careers in the Medical Laboratory
9650 Rockville Pike
Bethesda, Maryland 20014

National Institutes of Health Bureau of Health Manpower Education Information Office
9000 Rockville Pike
Bethesda, Maryland 20014

Public Inquiries
Health Services and Mental Health Administration
Public Health Service
Room 5-B-29
5600 Fishers Lane
Rockville, Maryland 20852

American Academy of Family Physicians
Volker Boulevard at Brookside
Kansas City, Missouri 64112

American Association of Industrial Nurses
79 Madison Avenue
New York, New York 10016

American College of Nurse-Midwifery
50 East 92nd Street
New York, New York 10028

American Heart Association
44 East 23rd Street
New York, New York 10010

American Medical Women's Association
1740 Broadway
New York, New York 10019

American Nurses Association
10 Columbus Circle
New York, New York 10019

ANA-NLNE Committee on Nursing Careers
10 Columbus Circle
New York, New York 10019

Maternity Center Association
48 East 92nd Street
New York, New York 10028

Appendix

National Association for Practical Nurse Education
and Services
1465 Broadway
New York, New York 10036

National Federation of Licensed Practical Nurses
250 West 57th Street
New York, New York 10019

National League for Nursing Education
10 Columbus Circle
New York, New York 10019

National Society for the Prevention of Blindness
79 Madison Avenue
New York, New York 10016

Planned Parenthood—World Population
810 Seventh Avenue
New York, New York 10019

American Academy of Physician's Associates
Duke University Medical Center
Box 2914 CHS
Durham, North Carolina 27706

Biologic Photographic Association
P. O. Box 12866
Philadelphia, Pennsylvania 19108

National Association of Certified Dental Laboratories
3801 Mount Vernon Avenue
Alexandria, Virginia 22305

National Association for Mental Health
1800 North Kent Street
Rosslyn, Virginia 22209

GLOSSARY OF TERMS AND ABBREVIATIONS

A.A.: Associate Arts degree

A.A.S.: Associate in Applied Science degree

accreditation: official endorsement of a college, university, or technical school.

A.M.A.: American Medical Association

A.N.A.: American Nurses Association

anesthesiology: the speciality of medicine involved in giving anesthetic agents to patients undergoing surgery.

cardiology: the branch of medicine that deals with heart disease.

C.C.U.: cardiac care unit

certification: insurance of the individual's satisfactory conclusion of a specific program. He must pass a written examination.

C.P.R.: cardio-pulmonary resuscitation

cytotechnology: the study of body cells

defibrillator: an electrical device employing two paddles that are placed on either side of the heart and through which an electric current is passed to stop heart fibrillations (wild, irregular rhythms) or to reactivate the heart during cardiac arrest.

E.R.: emergency room

electroencephalography: the study of brain waves to determine the presence of neural abnormalities.

geriatrics: the branch of medicine that deals with the aged.

gynecology: the diagnosis and treatment of diseases of the female reproductive organs.

Appendix

hematocrit: the ratio of red blood cells to whole blood; also the instrument used in determing this ratio.
hematology: the study of the blood
hemoglobin: the red pigment of the blood cell
histology: the study of tissues
I.C.U.: intensive care unit
intrapleural: within the thoracic cage (rib cage)
intrapulmonary: within the lung
I.V.: intravenous (within the veins)
leucocyte: white blood cell
licensure: the granting of a license by the state to an individual who has successfully passed an examination and has met the state's requirements for the practice of his profession.
M.E.T.: medical emergency technician
microbiology: the biological examination of microscopic organisms
nebulizer: an atomizer that dispenses a medicinal solution in the form of a fine spray to relieve chest congestion.
neurology: that specialty of medicine concerned with the diagnosis and treatment of diseases affecting the brain and nervous system.
N.L.N.E.: National League for Nursing Education
obstetrics: the specialty of medicine relating to childbirth and the care of the mother-to-be through pregnancy and birth and postnatal period.
ophthalmology: the specialty of medicine relating to the eye and its diseases.
O.R:. operating room
orthopedics: the medical specialty concerned with diseases and injuries to the bone
O.T.: occupational therapist

otolaryngology: the treatment of ear, nose, and throat diseases

O.T.R.: occupational therapy rehabilitation

pacemaker: a device (sometimes nuclear-powered) implanted in a patient's chest that stimulates the heartbeat with an electric current.

parasite: an organism living within or on another organism and taking food from it.

pathology: a clinical science using laboratory methods to discover the causes of disease within the body.

pediatrics: the branch of medicine that deals with infants and children.

pleura: the membrane that lines the thoracic cavity and the lung

pneumothorax: collapsed lung

prophylactic: guarding from or preventing disease

psychiatry: the diagnosis and treatment of mental illness

pulmonary: referring to the lung

radiology: the use of X-ray and radioactive material to study, diagnose, and treat diseases.

renal: referring to the kidneys

R.N.: registered nurse

stat: hospital jargon for "immediately"

urology: the diagnosis and treatment of urinary diseases and of the reproductive organs of the male

Index

A

Abbreviations, medical, 11
Accreditation. *See also* License, Certification.
Accreditation of nursing schools, 17
Activity in a hospital, 12
Administrator, hospital, 121
Alliance for Engineering in Medicine and Biology, 120
American Academy of Environmental Engineers, 119
American Academy of Family Physicians, 108
American Academy of Pediatrics, 108
American Art Therapy Association, 58
American Association of Colleges of Pharmacy, 117
American Association of Dental Schools, 74
American Association for Inhalation Therapy, 36
American Association of Medical Record Technicians, 66
American Association of Ophthalmology, 106
American Board of Orthopedic Surgery, 107
American Board of Thoracic Surgery, 103
American College of Hospital Administration, 122
American College of Obstetricians and Gynecologists, 107
American College of Radiology, 107
American College of Surgeons, 107
American Dental Association, 74
American Dental Hygienists Association, 65
American Diabetes Association, 108
American Dietetic Association, 63
American Heart Association, 108
American Home Economic Association, 63
American Hospital Association, 122
American Medical Association, 69, 86
American Medical Women's Association, 89
American Nurses Association, 17
American Occupational Therapy Association, 57, 58
American Optometric Association, 72
American Pharmaceutical Association, 117
American Podiatry Association, 112
American Psychiatric Association, 49, 106
American Psychological Association, 50
American Physical Therapy Association, 53
American Public Health Association, 106, 115
American Registry of Inhalation Therapists, 36
American Registry of Radiologic Technicians, 62
American Rehabilitation Counseling Association, 53
American Social Health Association, 50, 115
American Society of Anesthesiologists, 108
American Society of Clinical Pathologists, 107
American Society of Hospital Pharmacists, 117
American Society of Internal Medicine, 106
American Society for Pharmacology

139

and Experimental Therapeutics, 108, 117
American Society of Radiologic Technicians, 62
American Speech and Hearing Association, 56
American Statistical Association, 113
Anesthesiology, 101
Aspira for Puerto Ricans, 20
Assistant
  dietician, 64
  occupational therapy, 58
  physical therapy, 53
  physician's, 74
    duties, 76
    license, 77
    nursing base for, 76
    programs for, 77
    specialist, 76
  recreational therapy, 60
Associate Arts nursing degree, 17
Association of American Medical Colleges, 86, 106
Association of Operating Room Technicians, 69
Association of Schools of Allied Health Professions, 69
Association of University Programs in Hospital Administration, 122
Automation in the laboratory, 30

B

Bachelor of Science nursing degree, 17
Biomedical Engineering and Instrumentation Branch, National Institutes of Health, 121
Biomedical Engineering Society, 120
Biomedical equipment technician, 119
  organizations concerned with, 120
Blood bank, work of the, 25
Board of Certified Laboratory Assistants of the American Society of Medical Technologists, 27
Breakthrough for minority groups, 20
Breathing and respiration, 34

C

California Society of Psychiatric Technicians, 46, 49
Cardiac Surgeon, 103
Career guidance, 20
  for medical technologists, 31
  for minority groups, 20
Certification. See License, Accreditation.
Certified laboratory assistant, training for, 27
Chemistry laboratory, importance of the, 25
Childbirth, psychoprophylactic method of, 13
Choosing laboratory work, 27
City University of New York, 18
Community medicine, 18
Community mental health programs, 43
Computer technician, 120
Computerized laboratory work, 30
Consulting Service on Recreation for the Ill and Handicapped, 60
Coronary. See Heart.
Cost of medical education, 87
Council on Medical Education, 100
Council on Social Work Education, 48, 49
Cytology laboratory, work of the, 25
Cytotechnologist
  training for, 28
  work of the, 26

D

Dental hygienist, 64
Dentist, 73
  education of the, 73
  organizations concerned with the, 74
  specialists, 73
Dermatology, 101
Dietician, 62
  assistant to the, 64
  education of the, 63

Index

organizations concerned with the, 63
Diploma program for nursing, 17
Doctor. *See* Physician.

E

Ecology, working in field of, 117
Education
  cost of medical, 87
  dental, 73
  dietician's, 63
  for laboratory work, 27
  for mental health technician, 46
  nursing, 16
  for optometry, 72
  organizations concerned with, 89, 106
  for psychiatric social work, 48
  of the physical therapist, 53
  of the physician, 82
  for speech therapists, 55
  for X-ray technicians, 62
Emergency room technician, 66
  licenses for, 68
  organizations concerned with, 69
Engineer, sanitary, 119
Environmental technician, 117
  organizations concerned with, 118
Equipment and nurses, 15
Equipment technician, biomedical, 119
European Dialysis and Transplant Association, 105
Evaluation of self, 109

G

General practicioner, 101
Guidance
  career, 20
  for inhalation therapist, 37
  for medical technologists, 31
  for minority groups, 20
Gynecology and obstetrics, 101

H

Health career, selection of a, 109
Health centers, neighborhood, 21
Health statistician, public, 112
  organizations concerned with the, 112
Health teacher, 114
Hematology laboratory, importance of the, 24
Hippocratic Oath, 88
Histology laboratory, work of the, 26
Histology technician, training for, 28
Home-care programs in nursing, 21
Hospital. *See also* Medical.
  activity, 12
  administrator, 121
  organizations concerned with the, 122
  outreach programs, 18
  terminology, 11
Human Renal Transplant Registry, 105
Hygienist, dental, 64

I

Illness, mental, 42
Inhalation therapist
  career guidance for, 37
  educational requirements for, 36
  need for the, 35
  role of the, 33
  skills of the, 34
Institute of Food Technologists, 63
Intern, the medical, 97
Internal medicine, 100
International Association of Milk, Food and Environmental Sanitarians, 118, 119
Internship, rotating, 97

L

Laboratory
  automation in the, 30
  cytology, 25
  hematology, 24
  histology, 26
  importance of the, 25
  microbiology, 26
Laboratory assistant, training for certified, 27
Laboratory technologist. *See also* Medical technologist.
  specialization of the, 23
Laboratory work
  choosing, 27
  computerized, 30

education for, 27
importance of, 23
upgrading positions in, 27, 28, 29
License. *See also* Certification, Accreditation.
for emergency room technicians, 68
for operating room technicians, 69
for physician's assistant, 77
for podiatrist, 111
for practical nursing, 17

M

Maimonides Medical Center, 43
Medical. *See also* Hospital.
abbreviations, 11
education, organizations concerned with, 106
emergency technician. *See* Emergency room technician.
interns, 97
record technician, 65
education of, 66
records, importance of, 65
residents, 98
schools, 89
specialization, 98, 100
technologist
career guidance for, 31
needs for, 30
training of, 29
types of, 23
Medical College Admission Test, 86
Medicine
community, 18
internal, 100
space, 105
Mental health
community programs, 43
technicians, 42
duties of, 44
education of, 46
need for, 44
organizations concerned with, 49
Mental illness, 42
Microbiology laboratory, work of the, 26

Microtechnologist, work of the, 26
Midwives, nurses as, 15
Milieu therapy, 42
Minority groups
breakthrough for, 20
career guidance for, 20
Mount Sinai Hospital, 18

N

National Association for Mental Health, 50
National Association of Psychiatric Technicians, 46
National Association for Retarded Children, 50
National Australian Renal Transplantation Subcommittee, 105
National Commission for Social Work Careers, 50
National Environmental Health Association, 118, 119
National Institutes of Health, 50
National League for Nursing Education, 17
National Medical Association, 107
National Medical Fellowships, 89
National Medical Fellowships for Black Students, 107
National Merit Scholarship Corporation, 108
National Recreation and Park Association, 60
National Rehabilitation Counseling Association, 53
National Therapeutic Recreation Society, 60
Neighborhood health centers, 21
Neurology, 101
Nuclear-medicine technologist, 61
Nurses
and equipment, 15
as midwives, 15
needs for, 15, 16
pediatric, 16
psychiatric, 16
urban public health, 18
Nursing
as base for physician's assistant, 76
degree, Associate Arts, 17
degree, Bachelor of Science, 17

Index

diploma program for, 17
education, types of, 16
home-care programs in, 21
licensed practical, 17
organizations, 21
as a profession, 15
psychiatric, 48
rewards of, 21
specialization, 15
  variety in, 16
state boards of, 17
Nursing school
  accreditation of, 17
  selection of, 17

O

Obstetrics and gynecology, 101
Occupational therapist, 57
  assistant, 58
  organizations concerned with, 58
Operating room technician, 68
  license for, 69
  organizations concerned with, 69
Opthalmology, 102
Optometrist, 70
  education of the, 72
  organizations concerned with the, 72
Organizations concerned with
  biomedical equipment technicians, 120
  dentists, 74
  dieticians, 63
  environmental technicians, 118
  health statisticians, 113
  hospital administrators, 122
  medical education, 89, 106
  mental health workers, 49
  nurses, 21
  occupational therapy, 58
  operating and emergency room technicians, 69
  optometry, 72
  pharmacists, 117
  recreational therapy, 60
  rehabilitation work, 53
  sanitarians, 119
  speech therapy, 56
  teaching health, 115
  transplant surgery, 105
  X-ray technicians, 62
Orthopedics, 102

Outreach programs, hospital, 18

P

Paramedical personnel. See Physician's assistant.
Pathology, 102
Pediatric nurses, 16
Pediatrics, 101
Pharmacist, 116
  organizations concerned with the, 117
Physical therapist, 51
  assistant, 53
  education of the, 53
  See also Rehabilitation.
Physician
  in ancient times, the, 80
  cost of education of the, 87
  education of the, 82
Physician's assistant, 74
  duties of the, 76
  license for, 77
  nursing as a base for, 76
  programs for the, 77
  specialization of the, 76
Plastic surgery, 102
Podiatrist, 111
Podiatry schools, 111
Psychiatric care, 42
Psychiatric nurses, 16, 43
Psychiatric social worker, 47, 48
Psychiatric technicians, organizations of, 46
  See also Mental health technician.
Psychiatry, 102
Public health nurse, urban, 18
Public health statistician, 112
Puerto Ricans, Aspira for, 20

R

Radiologic technologist. See X-ray technician.
Radiology, 102
Records, importance of medical, 65
Recreation therapist, 59
  assistant to the, 60
  organizations concerned with the, 60
Registry of Medical Rehabilitation Therapists and Specialists, 53

Rehabilitation. *See also* Physical therapist.
  organizations involved in work of, 53
  personnel, 51
Resident, the medical, 98, 100
Rotating internship, 97

S

Sanitarian, the, 118
  organizations concerned with the, 119
Sanitary engineer, 119
Schools, accreditation of nursing, 17
  podiatry, 111
  medical, 89
  selection of nursing, 17
Science Talent Search, 107
Selection of health career, 109
Self, evaluation of, 109
Skills of the inhalation therapist, 34
Sloan Institute of Hospital Administration, 122
Social worker, psychiatric, 47
  education of the, 48
Society of Nuclear Medical Technologists, 62, 108
Society for Public Health Education, 113, 115
Society of Public Health Educators, 116
Space medicine, 105
Specialists
  dental, 73
  medical, 98, 100
  physician's assistants, 76
Specialization
  of the laboratory technologist, 23
  in nursing, 15, 16
Speech therapist, 54
  education of the, 55
  organizations concerned with the, 56
State board of nursing, 17
Statistician
  organizations concerned with the health, 113
  public health, 112
Surgeon
  cardiac, 103
  transplant, 104
Surgery
  organizations concerned with transplant, 105
  plastic, 102

T

Teacher, health, 114
  organizations concerned with the, 115
Technician
  biomedical equipment, 119
  computer, 120
  emergency room, 66
  environmental, 117
  histology, 28
  laboratory, 23
  medical, 23, 29, 30, 31
  medical record, 65, 66
  mental health, 42, 44, 46
  nuclear-medicine, 61
  operating room, 68
  psychiatric, 46
  X-ray, 61, 62, 63
Terminology, hospital, 11
Therapist
  inhalation, 33
  need for the, 53
  occupational, 58
  physical, 51, 53
  recreation, 59, 60
  speech, 54, 56
Therapy, milieu, 42
Transplant surgeon, 104
Transplant surgery, organizations concerned with, 105

U

Upgrading in laboratory work, 27, 28, 29
Urban public health nurse, the, 18
Urology, 103

V

Vogelbank Computing Center of Northwestern University, 105

X

X-ray technician, 61, 62
  education for, 62
  organizations concerned with the, 62